D1567515

Battle Orders • 25

US Airborne Divisions in the ETO 1944–45

Steven J Zaloga

Consultant Editor Dr Duncan Anderson • *Series editors* Marcus Cowper and Nikolai Bogdanovic

First published in Great Britain in 2007 by Osprey Publishing,
Midland House, West Way, Botley, Oxford OX2 0PH, UK
443 Park Avenue South, New York, NY 10016, USA
E-mail: info@ospreypublishing.com

A CIP catalogue record for this book is available from the British Library

ISBN 978 1 84176 118 2

Editorial by Ilios Publishing Ltd (www.iliospublishing.com)
Page layout by Boundford.com, Huntingdon. UK
Index by Alison Worthington
Typeset in GillSans and Stone Serif
Originated by United Graphics, Singapore
Printed in China through Bookbuilders

07 08 09 10 11   10 9 8 7 6 5 4 3 2 1

FOR A CATALOG OF ALL BOOKS PUBLISHED BY OSPREY MILITARY AND
AVIATION PLEASE CONTACT:

NORTH AMERICA
Osprey Direct, c/o Random House Distribution Center, 400 Hahn Road,
Westminster, MD 21157
E-mail: info@ospreydirect.com

ALL OTHER REGIONS
Osprey Direct UK, P.O. Box 140 Wellingborough, Northants, NN8 2FA, UK
E-mail: info@ospreydirect.co.uk
www.ospreypublishing.com

Author's note

The author would like to thank the staff of the US Army's Military
History Institute at the Army War College at Carlisle Barracks,
PA, for their kind assistance in the preparation of this book.
Thanks also go to Peter Brown and Timm Haasler for help with
several research questions. The photos in this book are primarily
from the wartime US Army's Signal Corps collections located
formerly at the Pentagon and the Defense Audio-Visual Agency
at Anacostia Navy Yard, and now at the US National Archives in
College Park, MD. Other Signal Corps and US Army photos were
located at other army facilities including the Military History
Institute, the US Military Academy at West Point, New York, the
Patton Museum, Fort Knox, Kentucky, and the Ordnance Museum,
Aberdeen Proving Ground, Maryland.

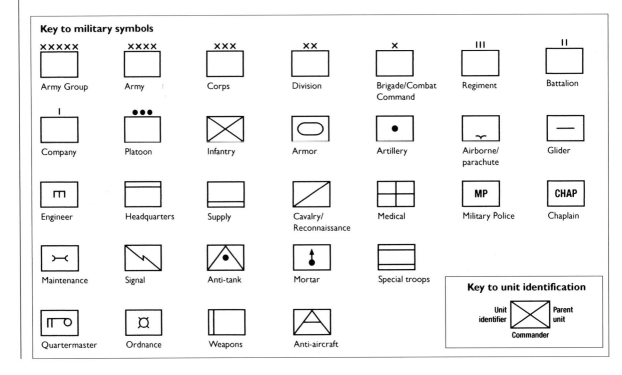

Key to military symbols

Army Group	Army	Corps	Division	Brigade/Combat Command	Regiment	Battalion
Company	Platoon	Infantry	Armor	Artillery	Airborne/ parachute	Glider
Engineer	Headquarters	Supply	Cavalry/ Reconnaissance	Medical	Military Police	Chaplain
Maintenance	Signal	Anti-tank	Mortar	Special troops		
Quartermaster	Ordnance	Weapons	Anti-aircraft			

Key to unit identification

Unit identifier — Parent unit — Commander

Introduction

By the end of World War II, the US Army deployed the largest airborne force in the world, created in barely three years. Airborne operations were a revolutionary tactic that transcended the limits of traditional linear land warfare by conducting combat missions deep in the enemy rear through the use of airlift. During the final year of the war, the US Army conducted four airborne operations in the ETO. The airborne drops behind Utah Beach on D-Day were a tactical disappointment due to the wide dispersion of the airborne units after a confused night drop. In spite of this the mission was an operational success since it managed to disrupt the German defenses even if not in the fashion intended. Operation *Dragoon* in southern France on August 15, 1944, was the smallest of these operations and the least consequential since German resistance in the area was so weak. The boldest of the missions, Operation *Market* in September 1944, was part of a larger British scheme to seize a bridgehead over the Rhine at Arnhem. Although the overall mission failed, the two US airborne divisions taking part fulfilled their tactical objectives in a clear demonstration of the potential of airborne operations. The final airborne mission of the war, Operation *Varsity* in March 1945, was the best executed of the wartime airborne missions and spearheaded the British advance over the Rhine. Ultimately, the airborne divisions never lived up to their revolutionary promise. Airborne operations proved to be extremely complex to conduct and were too few in number to substantially affect the course of the campaigns in Northwest Europe. Yet the combat performance of the US airborne divisions was so outstanding that they have become a fixture in the US Army ever since.

"Where is the Prince who can afford so to cover his country with troops for its defense, as that ten thousand men descending from the clouds, might not, in many places, do an infinite deal of mischief before a force could be brought

A dramatic scene from Landing Zone W on September 23, 1944, during Operation *Market* with CG-4A gliders of recently landed elements of the 101st Airborne Division in the foreground while in the background, the C-47 transports of the 315th Troop Carrier Group drop elements of the 1st Polish Parachute Brigade on Drop Zone O near Overasselt. (NARA)

together to repel them?" So wrote one of America's "founding fathers," Benjamin Franklin in 1784, in a remarkably futuristic vision of warfare by balloon. In France in 1918, another visionary, Gen. Billy Mitchell, convinced Gen. Pershing to begin plans to drop an entire division of troops from bombers to take the fortress city of Metz from the air. The war ended before the plans could take shape. But curiously enough, the officer assigned the task of studying this project was Lewis Brereton, who would lead the US airborne force a quarter century later.

When the idea of airborne troops was revived some 20 years later, the initial debate focused on who would actually train and command the force. The US Army's Chief of Infantry proposed the creation of a small air infantry force in March 1939 as the "Marines of the Air Corps," or "air grenadiers." The engineers argued that they should be placed under their control since their primary mission initially was seen as rear area demolition and sabotage. The War Department's G-3 section wanted them placed under their control as a strategic reserve of the general headquarters. The Army Air Force (AAF) wanted them under their control since their aircraft would be an integral part in the operations.

The startling success of German paratroopers at Eben Emael in Belgium in May 1940 made clear the potential of airborne forces and helped ensure the establishment of a counterpart organization in the US Army. In August 1940, the US Army General Staff finally decided to leave the new "air infantry forces" under the Chief of Infantry. A test platoon was formed at Fort Benning in June 1940, expanded to a battalion in September 1940. Later German operations, such as the airborne assault on Crete in May 1941, suggested that airborne forces could conduct missions much more substantial than mere airborne raids. The US Army quickly absorbed these lessons and the infant airborne force expanded rapidly following the US entry into the war in December 1941.

In March 1942, the Provisional Parachute Group at Ft. Benning became a formal part of the Army Ground Forces (AGF) as the new Airborne Command. Col. William C. Lee, who had been instrumental in the formation of the first US airborne units, headed this organization. By the summer of 1942, the Airborne Command had four principal units: three parachute infantry regiments (501st, 502nd and 503rd) and one airborne (glider) infantry regiment (the 88th). Equally important, in April 1942, the AAF formed the Air Transport Command responsible for the delivery of parachute troops, airborne infantry and glider units. At the time, three methods of airborne delivery were considered viable: parachute, glider and airborne landing. The presumption was that paratroopers would be used in any operation as the spearhead to seize a landing zone for gliders or an enemy airstrip for air-landing troops. The idea of air-landing infantry troops behind enemy lines at a captured airfield was based on the German use of this tactic on Crete in 1941, and the idea of glider landings was inspired both by Eben Emael and Crete.

The US airborne did not have a centralized command structure comparable to the German XI Fliegerkorps, which combined both the air transport formations and air-landing troops under a single tactical organization. This was made simpler by the fact that both elements were part of the Luftwaffe, while in the American case the two elements were divided between the AAF and AGF. Although various schemes were put forward to better coordinate these two commands, the substantial difficulties of raising and training the new formations, as well as inter-service rivalries, diverted attention from this issue. By the time that US airborne divisions were ready for commitment in the ETO, the broader issue of the coordination of US troop carrier units and their British counterparts, as well as coordination of US and British airborne operations, had become a much more vital issue.

The original US airborne force was based around regiments, not divisions, on the assumption that this would provide greater flexibility in planning and executing missions. However, the Germans had evidently used divisions on

The Douglas C-47 Skytrain was the workhorse of the Army Air Force transport squadrons, and this restored example is displayed at the air museum at Le Bourget airfield in France. (Author's collection)

Crete and, by early 1942, the US Army was thinking along the same lines. At first, the AGF headquarters simply wanted to assign the airborne mission to normal infantry divisions that would receive additional training. However, airborne advocates strongly objected to this idea on the grounds that the infantry division organization was ill suited to air-landing operations and that the personnel would require too much specialized parachute training. By the summer of 1942, the consensus had reverted back to the idea of dedicated airborne divisions and Lee was dispatched to Great Britain to examine the British organization. Lee recommended the British mix of two parachute and one glider regiments per division, but the head of the AGF, Gen. Lesley McNair, preferred a mix of two glider and one parachute regiments. The argument over the balance of forces within the airborne was based partly on tactics and partly on economy. Parachute troops were seen as elite troops requiring more stringent recruitment practices and a much higher level of training. The regular infantry was wary of letting these units expand too much as there was the feeling that this would drain infantry units of highly motivated young troops who would otherwise serve as small unit tactical leaders in the regular infantry divisions. In contrast, glider infantry was not expected to require a high level of specialized individual training, and gliders were envisioned as cheap and reusable. From this perspective, the parachute regiment would serve as the spearhead to land and secure the landing zone, and would be followed by the glider regiments and perhaps some air-landed units as well. As a result, the first airborne divisions formed in August 1942, the 82nd and 101st Airborne Divisions, both had a mix of one parachute and two glider regiments. As we shall see, this issue would remain contentious through 1943–44.

Combat mission

The most obvious difference between airborne units and conventional infantry was the use of air transport to deliver the units into combat. This had important implications in their combat mission. In order to be air transportable, airborne infantry were invariably lighter armed than comparable infantry units and had much more limited logistical support. Since the airborne units would be landed at some depth behind enemy lines and fight in isolation for some time, these factors strongly shaped the missions assigned to airborne divisions. The role of these formations was envisioned as complete commitment by air, seizure of essential but limited objectives and quick relief by juncture with the associated main ground effort.

As a result of these factors, several missions were seen as particularly suitable for airborne operations, with two being the primary missions. The first mission was to seize, hold or otherwise exploit important tactical locations in conjunction with, or pending the arrival of, other forces. This was the primary mission executed by airborne divisions on D-Day in Normandy, Operation *Dragoon* in southern France in August 1944 and Operation *Market* in the Netherlands in September 1944. The second major mission envisioned for the airborne divisions was to attack the enemy rear and assist a breakthrough or landing by the main force. This mission was part of the assignment of the US airborne divisions on D-Day, but better describes the main mission of Operation *Varsity* in March 1945. There were several other missions envisioned for airborne divisions, some of which were subsidiary objectives for the operations conducted in 1944–45. At least four were outlined in various field manuals: to block or delay enemy reserves by capturing and holding key terrain features; to capture or destroy vital enemy installations thereby disrupting his

The German use of gliders at Eben Emael and Crete encouraged US development of this capability. This is a C-47 of the 90th TCS, 438th Troop Carrier Group, towing aloft a Horsa glider from Greenham Common on D-Day, June 6, 1944. (NARA)

system of command, communications and supply; to capture enemy airfields; and to delay a retreating enemy force.

Due to their dependence on air transport, air-landing tactics were unique to airborne infantry doctrine. One of the major issues in planning airborne missions was the matter of nighttime versus daytime drops. The US Army initially favored nighttime missions since it was presumed that the cover of darkness would shield the airborne landing at its most vulnerable moment. However, in practice, the difficulty of landing an airborne force with any precision led to a shift in policy after Normandy that restricted airborne operations to daylight missions to prevent the excessive dispersion of forces. Weather posed a similar dilemma to airborne forces. Due to the inadequacy of radio-electronic navigation aids in 1944–45, some degree of visual navigation was essential for both the troop transport pilots and the glider pilots. As a result, airborne missions were invariably limited by the weather to relatively clear days, or days where the cloud cover was high enough to permit the air trains to fly under it.

In spite of these distinct limitations, airborne missions possessed some significant advantages. Their most important asset was surprise. An airborne drop could take place anywhere, at any time, forcing the Germans to divert forces to defend against the vertical threat. For example, the threat of airborne attack forced the Germans to fortify the landward sides of key ports along the English Channel for fear they could be rapidly seized by a surprise airborne assault. Airborne missions could use the leverage provided by air delivery to avoid the strongest enemy defenses and attack the enemy where weakest, greatly amplifying the combat power of these otherwise lightly armed units.

On the other hand, airborne divisions had distinct limitations compared to conventional infantry divisions. Their infantry regiments were generally smaller, especially in regards to supporting weapons. Since their artillery had to be delivered by air, it was invariably less powerful—the 75mm pack howitzer versus the 105mm howitzer in the conventional divisions. Logistical support was minimal so the division could only fight for a few days before needing substantial reinforcement.

Since airborne divisions would often fight behind enemy lines, the capability to re-supply from the air was essential. This is a re-supply mission flown to the 101st Airborne Division in Bastogne by the 73rd Troop Carrier Squadron, 434th TCG, in December 1944. (NARA)

Preparation for war: doctrine and training

Lessons learned

By the time that the US airborne divisions took part in the campaigns in the ETO in 1944, experience had already been accumulated from earlier operations in the Mediterranean Theater in 1942–44. These earlier operations had a profound effect on the doctrine and training of the US airborne divisions, so a brief survey is essential.

The first mission was conducted by the 2/503rd Parachute Infantry Regiment (PIR) in French North Africa as part of Operation *Torch* on November 8, 1942. The operation was a bit of a mess as the mission was flown all the way from Britain to Morocco, a daunting flight under the best of circumstances, and the paratroopers were not certain whether they would land on undefended French airstrips near Oran or conduct a parachute jump against hostile forces. In the event, it was a mixture of both and the task force was unable to accomplish its mission. The force was then hastily assigned a mission to seize the Youks-les-Bains Airstrip and its large gasoline reserve on November 14, but jumped into the midst of a French battalion reinforced with armored cars. Fortunately, the French commander decided against resisting the landing, as otherwise the mission would have turned into a bloody shambles. A third mission was conducted on December 26, 1942, but was a small-scale raid involving three C-47 aircraft and 29 paratroopers assigned to blow up a key bridge in Tunisia. The teams were dropped at night, but could not find the bridge. The lessons of these early missions were obvious. Detailed planning was essential to the conduct of airborne missions; slap-dash, improvised planning was a recipe for disaster. The troop carrier units had to receive better training and joint training with airborne units; troop carrier command should not treat airborne missions as just another routine freight operation.

These lessons came at an opportune time, as plans were underway for the first large-scale airborne mission to support Operation *Husky*, the amphibious

Air-landing or gliders? The German landings on Crete convinced the US Army to explore the possibility of landing troops on captured runways as one possible air-delivery technique. Here, infantry troops and an M1A1 75mm pack howitzer are air delivered during wargames in North Carolina in 1942. (MHI)

Night or day drop? The hazards of night drops are all too evident in this scene from Normandy after D-Day with a shattered Horsa littering the landing zone, and a parachute caught in the tree. Planners finally concluded that German flak was less of a threat than the difficulties of night landing, and Operation *Market* in September 1944 was conducted in daylight. (NARA)

landings on Sicily in July 1943. Sicily was also the first joint Allied airborne operation, with the British 1st Airborne Division assigned to land near Syracuse to seize a key bridge and points south of the city, while elements of the US 82nd Airborne Division were to land behind the US Army beachhead at Gela to block the advance of Axis forces. The airborne drop on July 9, 1943, was widely dispersed due to navigation problems, landing in a swath over 50 miles, with only about 425 paratroopers of the initial 3,405 landing near Gela as planned.

In spite of the limited success of the mission, Sicily would be better remembered for the tragedy that ensued on the night of July 11 when an attempt was made to reinforce the original landing force with two battalions from the 504th PIR. The 82nd Airborne Division commander, Maj. Gen. Matthew Ridgway, thought the naval commanders off Sicily had been warned adequately about the approach of the airborne train. But the mission occurred shortly after a Luftwaffe bombing raid on the fleet and as a result, during the nighttime flight to the drop zone, the warships began firing on the C-47s, shooting down 23 aircraft and seriously damaging 37 more.

The lessons from the Sicily operation continued to focus on the relatively poor training of the troop carrier pilots, particularly the difficulties experienced in night drops. Cooperation between the AAF and AGF units continued to be poor, and an after-action assessment concluded that troop carrier capabilities for glider operations were "practically zero." Even though the Navy assured the Army that such costly fratricide would be avoided in the future by better planning, the Army became very wary of conducting nighttime missions that passed over the invasion fleet, as would be seen in the flight approach selected for the Normandy landings a year later.

The most important technical lesson was the need for improved navigation aids as well as greater attention to the use of simple routes, improved navigation training and improved nighttime formation flying. One of the immediate outcomes of the Sicily operation was the establishment of a pathfinder force, consisting of select transport squadrons with improved navigation equipment and experienced crews, and an associated paratrooper pathfinder unit that could be landed in advance of the main force to set up beacons and navigation aids for the main wave of the airborne assault.

Senior US commanders were so discouraged by the Sicily airborne operation that there was some thought of reorganizing the existing airborne divisions as light infantry divisions. The head of Army Ground Forces, Lt. Gen. Lesley McNair, commented that "after the airborne operations in Africa and Sicily, my staff and I had become convinced of the impracticality of handling large airborne units. I was prepared to recommend to the War Department that airborne divisions be abandoned in our scheme of organization and that the airborne effort be restricted to parachute units of battalion size or smaller." However, other commanders correctly pointed out that airborne operations were still in their infancy and that if important improvements were made in coordination and training, the divisions might live up to their potential. The AAF continued to be supportive of the concept but, more importantly, Gen. Dwight Eisenhower was keen on the idea of using airborne divisions in the forthcoming invasion of France planned for the summer of 1944.

Paradoxically, while the Allies were disappointed by the airborne operations, the Germans thought they had been an important success. In spite of their dispersion, the paratroopers wreaked havoc all along the front and the Italian Army estimated it had been assaulted by a force of 20,000 to 30,000 troops. The German commander, Field Marshal Albert Kesselring, acknowledged later that the paratroopers had caused unusual delays in the movement of reserves and the head of the German paratrooper force, Gen. Kurt Student, was even more effusive in his praise, stating that the Hermann Göring Panzer Division would have hurled the invasion force back into the sea were it not for the effective delay imposed by the paratroopers.

The last major airborne operation prior to D-Day was in support of the Allied landings at Salerno in September 1943. The Wehrmacht launched a mechanized counter-offensive that threatened to split the beachhead, and the Fifth Army commander, Gen. Mark Clark, requested an airborne reinforcement as quickly as possible. Within 15 hours, some 1,300 paratroopers of the 82nd Airborne Division were successfully dropped into the beachhead area on September 13, reinforced the following night by another regiment. Although the reinforcement mission was highly successful, many paratrooper officers wondered about the value of reinforcing a beachhead with highly trained paratroopers when they might have been used more effectively landing behind German lines. A final mission was conducted on the night of September 14–15,

Gliders were expected to be a cost-effective means of airborne delivery since it was presumed they would be re-usable. In reality, damage was often severe enough that they became disposable, and at a unit cost similar to a Sherman tank, not inexpensive. Here, a CG-4A is seen in the landing zone at La Motte, France, while another CG-4A prepares to land during Operation *Dragoon* on August 15, 1944. (MHI)

A significant advantage of gliders was their ability to carry heavier loads that were awkward for parachute delivery. Here, troops of Battery A, 320th Glider Field Artillery Battalion, 82nd Airborne Division, practice loading a 75mm M1A1 pack howitzer aboard a CG-4A glider near Oujda, Morocco, during training in July 1943. (MHI)

landing the 2/509th PIR near a mountain pass 20 miles north of Salerno with the intention of blocking it. The mission was hastily planned and the troop carriers became badly dispersed on the approach to the drop zone. The 640 paratroopers were scattered over a 100 square miles of terrain. Although they were unable to conduct their planned mission, they harassed German forces and about 510 troops managed to make their way back to Allied lines. It was another reminder of the challenge of night drops given inadequate aircrew training and the limited navigation technologies of the time.

One of the major doctrinal questions not answered by the early combat operations was the ideal mix of paratroop versus glider units. This could not be settled as there had been delays in the production of gliders which limited training and deployment. Initially, the AGF favored a higher percentage of glider battalions over paratroop battalions, as the glider troops did not require specialized jump training and the gliders promised to be cheap and re-useable. From a tactical perspective, the early combat drops demonstrated the tendency of paratroop units to become badly scattered, leading to poor unit assembly and failed missions. Gliders promised to circumvent these problems since the unit arrived intact at the small unit (squad) level, and there was some hope that dispersion could be better controlled. In addition, gliders made it possible to land larger equipment such as jeeps, light artillery and supplies in a more convenient fashion than parachute. On the other hand, gliders took up more air time for delivery of a unit due to the spacing requirements of the gliders and the need for more relaxed formation flying to prevent mid-air collisions between tow planes and gliders. Time was a critical ingredient in airborne operations since the enemy forces were alerted once the drops began and anti-aircraft fire increased once surprise was lost. The early operations were conducted as single tows, with each C-47 towing a single CG-4A glider. It was hoped that training would improve to the point where double tows would be possible, which would help reduce the time delays of glider operations.

Training

From the outset, the US Army realized that paratroop units would have to be manned by troops a cut above average in all respects. Jumping out of an aircraft at low altitude on a pitch-dark night, burdened with nearly 100lb of gear, and being ready to fight on reaching the ground were extreme demands not expected of ordinary infantry conscripts. Furthermore, paratroop operations often resulted in small units being widely scattered, and the troops needed a high degree of self-motivation and initiative to carry out their mission. From the outset, paratroopers were volunteers, which helped to narrow down the recruitment process. The Army offered other incentives such as an additional $50 per month in jump pay ($100 for officers). Besides the financial incentives, many adventurous young soldiers were attracted by the allure of joining an elite combat force, and esprit de corps was consciously fostered by the paratroop commanders by distinguishing the paratroopers from regular infantry troops with modified battledress, jump boots and distinctive insignia.

Most individual paratroop training was similar to the normal 13-week infantry training with the exception of jump training. Jump school at Ft. Benning was a four-week course, starting with tower jumps and culminating in five parachute jumps from aircraft, the last of which was a night jump.[1] In spite of

1 For further details see Carl Smith *Warrior 26: US Paratroope 1941–45* (Osprey: Oxford, 2000)

the additional jump training, the head of AGF, Gen. McNair, was very concerned about the tactical training in "trick" divisions such as these, fearing that concentration on the "trick" training would lead to slack standards in regular tactical training. Yet McNair's concerns were largely misplaced. In combat, the excellent training and esprit de corps of the paratroopers helped to overcome the shortcomings in the tactics and divisional organization

In contrast to the paratroopers, little separated the glider infantry, or "glider riders" as they were sometimes called, from ordinary infantry. They did not receive jump training, their equipment was essentially the same as regular infantry, and they did not receive any hazardous duty pay. Indeed, the distinct differences in treatment between the glider infantry and the paratroop infantry in the airborne divisions fostered a great deal of resentment in the glider ranks. A poster appeared at one of the army air bases with gruesome photos of several glider wrecks and the slogan: "Join the Glider Troops! No Flight Pay, No Jump Pay, But—Never a Dull Moment." The situation became serious enough that on July 1, 1944, after the D-Day operations, the Army reversed its policy and awarded extra glider pay.

Paratroopers of Co. H, 513th PIR, 17th Airborne Division, practice on March 5, 1945, prior to Operation *Varsity*. This was the only unit to make combat jumps from the larger C-46 Commando aircraft, which had a pair of doors on either side instead of the C-47's single door, necessitating additional training. (NARA)

Glider pilots were in a somewhat different position as they were recruited and trained by the AAF. Initial attempts to recruit pilots with civilian flight experience had to be abandoned since there was such a large demand for experienced pilots by the AAF and Navy and eventually the physical requirements for glider pilots had to be lowered to recruit enough pilots. Glider pilots went through basic training with the AAF Flying Training Command and then were assigned to Troop Carrier Command for operational training. They were classified as flying officers—not commissioned officers but not enlisted men either. Once the specialized glider training was completed, the glider pilots were then assigned to the Troop Carrier Groups and sent to one of the airbases specializing in airborne training, such as Pope Field, Laurinburg-Maxton Airbase or Lawson Field, for additional joint training. As in the case of transport pilots, they were expected to fly at least four hours per month to retain their added flight pay. One of the lingering controversies over glider pilot training was whether they should receive individual infantry training. AAF policy was

A number of exercises were conducted in 1942–43 to test new tactics. Here, a combination parachute drop and air-landing exercise is conducted at Ft. Bragg, North Carolina, in 1942. (NARA)

Glider pilots and co-pilots were recruited and trained by the Army Air Force. Here, the 442nd Troop Carrier Group conducts a practice CG-4A glider mission in France in February 1945 prior to Operation *Varsity*. (NARA)

that once the pilot landed the glider during a combat operation, he was to be evacuated back to the airbase as expeditiously as possible. The AAF did not want to expend highly trained pilots as infantry. However, there was some concern that once the gliders landed, the idle glider pilots would be more of a hindrance than a help in the airborne operation if they had to be defended by the glider infantry. Although there was an effort to rectify this situation prior to D-Day, in practice the glider pilots received no formal infantry training while stationed in the US. In some units stationed near airborne divisions in Britain, airborne officers provided limited training. As mentioned later, this policy changed in 1944 based on the lessons of the airborne operations.

Troop carrier pilots were trained much the same as other AAF pilots, starting in Flying Training Command and then progressing to Troop Carrier Command for unit training. This training included both the dropping of paratroopers as well as glider tug training. Considerable emphasis was placed on night flying, since it was presumed that much of the combat flying would be conducted under the cover of darkness. There were plans underway to establish a special training area in the Great Lakes area with live anti-aircraft gun corridors to familiarize the crews with the disturbing presence of flak tracer in night flying, but this was never put into effect. In spite of the demands of the job, Troop Carrier Command did not receive priority for pilots and indeed the high demand for combat pilots led to the reduction in physical requirements for the troop carriers. An AAF jibe about pilot selection was that "many are called, few are chosen, and the rest end up in Troop Carrier." Troop Carrier Command became a dumping ground for below-average washouts from four-engine bomber training. The commanders of Troop Carrier Command tried to reverse this attitude among senior AAF commanders as they recognized that their pilots were being tasked with some of the most demanding and difficult missions of the war—flying unarmed aircraft at altitudes of under 1,000ft, at speeds over the drop zone of only 120 miles per hour, in tight formations where it was forbidden to take evasive action even in the presence of flak. To further degrade morale, the standard C-47 transport aircraft was not fitted with self-sealing fuel tanks, which made it especially vulnerable to the type of light flak so often encountered over the drop zones. Limitations in available C-47 transport aircraft and rationing of fuel during stateside training through much of 1943 made it difficult at some bases for pilots to reach the mandatory four hours per month flying time, though this situation eased once the units forward deployed to Britain. To further complicate training, many of the flight configurations planned for the troop carriers had never been demonstrated. Double tows of CG-4A gliders did not take place on a significant scale until mid-1943, and the first aerial re-supply with door-delivered and para-pack containers was not demonstrated until December 1943. The plan was to have two crews per aircraft, but by D-Day this objective was not close to being met and there was generally only a single crew per aircraft. In many groups there was only one navigator per three aircraft but the AAF hoped to cover this deficiency by relying on tight group formations.

Large-scale joint exercises of the airborne divisions and troop carrier groups were an extremely complicated and costly undertaking. The special board headed by Maj. Gen. Joseph Swing in 1943 recommended that each division conduct at least 13 weeks of unit training and then follow this by 12 weeks of joint training with the Troop Carrier Command. The new directive for airborne training in October 1943 reduced the Swing Board recommendation from 12 weeks of combined training to eight, with the first four-week period emphasizing small-unit training such as loading, landing, assembly and entry into combat by company, with the troop carriers practicing at squadron level. The second phase would be battalion combat teams and troop carrier groups, and the final one week phase would be a major maneuver by the division and wing, moving the division in two lifts. The first large-scale joint training operation was conducted in May 1943 during the Carolina wargames by the 101st Airborne Division, moving 7,000 troops in 32 hours using three troop carrier groups. The exercise uncovered problems in the glider operations which forced more attention to be paid to air discipline and training. McNair was critical of the performance of the 101st Airborne Division in the exercise and emphasized the need for more attention to ground combat training. The largest joint exercise in the US prior to D-Day was conducted in December 1943 involving the 53rd Wing and 11th Airborne Division in the Carolinas, delivering 10,282 troops in 39 hours. The breakdown was 4,679 by parachute, 1,869 by glider and 3,734 air landed at a "captured" airport. This exercise demonstrated that problems uncovered in the May 1943 exercise had been cleared up and that double glider tow, one of the more difficult tactical problems, could now be accepted as "routine." These large-scale exercises were of particular importance to the airborne and troop carrier staffs in ironing out the considerable problems of conducting complex airborne operations, and were an important step in the final planning for airborne operations on D-Day. Once in England, joint training tended to intensify, indeed to the point where the airborne divisions started to resist further training in the late spring due to "overtraining" and the risk of injury to trained troops. The largest and last major joint exercise prior to D-Day was Exercise Eagle starting on May 11, 1944. The results of the paratroop drops were excellent except for the less experienced new arrivals such as 315th and 442nd TCG. The glider exercises revealed lingering problems leading to "a mixture of opposition and fatalistic resignation" according to one official history.

Unit organization

The rifleman's standard weapon in the airborne was the same as in the regular infantry, the M1 Garand rifle. This is Lt. Kelso Horne, leader of the 1st Platoon, Co. I, 508th PIR of the 82nd Airborne Division near St. Saveur-le-Vicomte in mid-June after the Normandy landings. (NARA)

The US Army airborne divisions were originally organized under the October 1942 table of organization (TO&E) around two glider infantry regiments and one parachute infantry regiment. Two changes were instituted to this table in October 1943 and February 1944, and the table shown on page 18 is based on the February 24, 1944, version that was in effect at the time of D-Day. The divisional organization was heavily influenced by the preferences of the chief of the AGF, Gen. Lesley McNair, who favored the smallest organization possible to make it easier to ship the units overseas. McNair preferred to add capabilities to an austere divisional structure by overseas attachments rather than incorporate them as organic elements of the divisional tables. However, this tendency often got carried away. So for example, the glider infantry regiment had only two battalions, instead of the triangular organization elsewhere in the infantry, causing tactical problems. The skimpy organization also was based on the false presumption that War Department doctrine would be followed and that airborne divisions would be relieved a few days after landing. In practice, it was difficult to extract a high-value combat formation from the midst of battle across crowded lines of communication, and the airborne divisions invariably fought for weeks rather than days before relief. This skeletal structure proved so troublesome under actual combat conditions that there were continual efforts to circumvent the tables of organization and add assets.

In comparison to regular infantry regiments, the airborne regiments in June 1944 had fewer troops and weapons, and were roughly half the size. Due to the limitations of air delivery, the divisional structure was considerably more austere than a comparable infantry division, with significantly less artillery firepower and a much more skeletal logistical infrastructure. The infantry

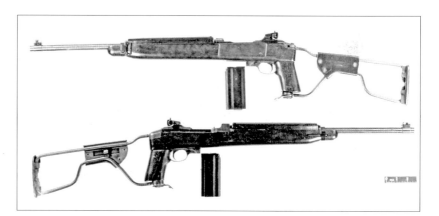

The standard sidearm in the airborne was a folding-stock version of the M1A1 .30-cal. carbine. (MHI)

division had three 105mm howitzer battalions for direct support and one 155mm howitzer battalion for general support while the airborne division had three 75mm pack howitzer battalions, one delivered by parachute and two by glider. Although the airborne division was authorized a modest number of trucks for supply, these could not be delivered by air and so were only available at base, or during prolonged ground operations. The only vehicle other than motor scooters that could be air delivered was the 1/4-ton truck (jeep), which was the mainstay of the airborne division for tactical requirements. In place of trucks, the units were issued with handcarts to assist in moving ammunition and supplies. Some tactical units were omitted and the division lacked a reconnaissance element and a military police formation, which forced the diversion of airborne infantry to take on these functions in the combat zone.

The divisional organization was especially bare in regards to administrative and support personnel. It lacked an organic parachute maintenance capability, which became more noticeable once deployed overseas than when the divisions were stationed in the US. Its small allotment of tactical vehicles adversely affected training and administration of the division when not in combat. To make up for these shortfalls, airborne divisions tended to have an abnormally large number of attachments when the division was involved in prolonged ground combat. These are detailed below in the "Unit status" section where the key attachments in several of the major operations are listed. However, corps commanders during the war were not happy with this arrangement as it drained the corps of combat battalions and support units needed for corps operations. In addition, corps commanders frequently complained that the airborne divisions did not make best use of attached combat units such as tank battalions as they had generally not trained with such units and were unfamiliar with their tactical employment. They were also critical of the airborne divisions' lack of skill in using attached quartermaster truck units,

Airborne troops carried as much ammunition and supplies as was practical as seen here with a paratrooper armed with an M1A1 Thompson .45-cal. sub-machine gun with numerous extra magazines after a practice jump in France in February 1945. (MHI)

Besides the jeep, the only other motor vehicle delivered during airdrops in any number was the airborne motor scooter. This example is the standard Cushman Model 53, weighing 260lb with a 5hp engine. The US Army acquired a total of 4,734 in 1944–45 primarily for airborne use. (MHI)

Troops of the 101st Airborne Division move down a road in Normandy following the airdrops. The small number of tactical vehicles in the division obliged airborne units to employ handcarts to move supplies and ammunition as seen here. (NARA)

once again due to their unfamiliarity with standard infantry practices. The use of attachments rather than organic components proved to be a poor concept and was abandoned after the war. The changes in the divisional tables through 1944 tried to add a minimum number of formations to clear up the worst of the problems.

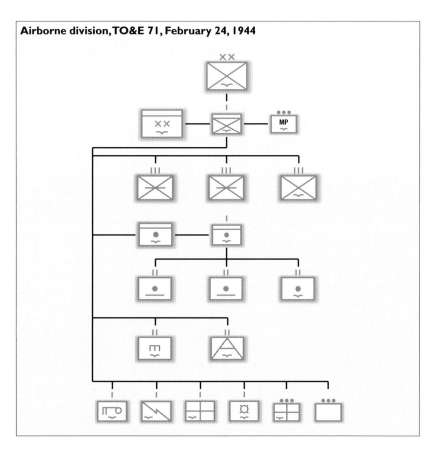

Airborne division, TO&E 71, February 24, 1944

The actual airborne divisional structure was much less rigid than the regular infantry divisions due to the novelty of the doctrine and its basic immaturity. Improvements were continually taking place, many of them outside the table of organization. Prior to Operation *Husky* on Sicily, the 82nd Airborne Division had adopted a mix of two parachute and one glider infantry regiments due to shortages of gliders. This mix remained the preferred divisional configuration in spite of the tables of organization. Prior to the Normandy landings, the 82nd Airborne Division's 504th PIR was committed to the Anzio operation in Italy and was unable to rejoin the division in time for Normandy. In January, the division was allotted the 507th and 508th PIR, which were added to the veteran 505th PIR and the 325th GIR, giving the division a four-regiment structure with a preponderance of parachute regiments instead of the intended glider-heavy configuration. As a result, the 82nd Airborne Division also had four artillery battalions instead of the usual three. Furthermore, the glider infantry regiment was reinforced with another battalion to conform to the US Army's doctrinal preference for a triangular regiment instead of the two-battalion organization called for under the existing table. Likewise, the 101st Airborne shifted to a mix favoring parachute regiments, adding the 506th PIR and attaching the 501st PIR in addition to its 502nd PIR and 327th GIR, and also receiving a third battalion for its glider infantry regiment. There were also numerous changes from the table of equipment. For example, the February 1944 table authorized the use of the obsolete 37mm anti-tank gun as the division's only anti-tank artillery since the standard infantry division weapon, the 57mm gun, was too heavy. However, prior to D-Day, the 82nd and 101st Airborne Divisions were both able to obtain

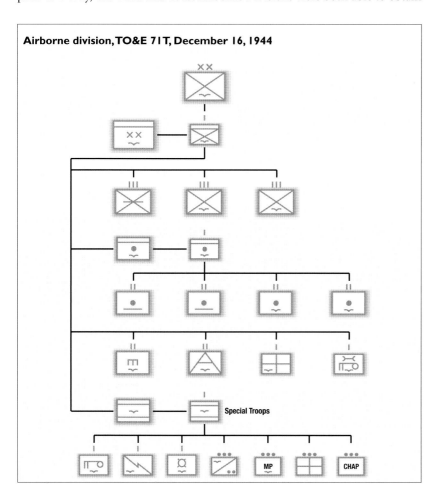

Airborne division, TO&E 71T, December 16, 1944

Special Troops

	HQ & HQ co.	MP platoon	Divisional artillery	Parachute infantry regiment	Glider infantry regt. (x2)	Engineer bn.
Officers	49	2	102	136	70	26
Enlisted men	152	36	1,365	1,818	1,538	401
Parachute	0	0	431	1,749	0	139
.45-cal. pistol	19	1	48	10	8	2
.30-cal. carbine	172	33	1,420	717	766	170
.30-cal. rifle	0	0	0	1,227	792	255
.45-cal. SMG	0	4	0	54	36	18
.30-cal. BAR	0	0	0	0	42	0
.30-cal. LMG	0	2	0	132	12	21
.30-cal. HMG	0	0	0	0	8	0
2.36in. bazooka	10	0	177	73	73	25
.50-cal. HMG	3	0	56	4	3	0
60mm mortar	0	0	0	27	24	0
81mm mortar	0	0	0	12	12	0
37mm AT gun	0	0	4	0	8	0
75mm howitzer	0	0	36	0	0	0
M3A4 handcart	0	0	0	27	72	20
M6A1 handcart	0	0	20	0	0	0
Motor scooter	4	0	46	52	29	20
Motorcycle	0	2	0	0	0	0
1/4-ton jeep	9	4	97	15	20	19
3/4-ton truck	5	8	3	1	0	0
2 1/2-ton truck	10	0	27	16	10	4
1/4-ton trailer	1	4	35	10	12	8
1-ton trailer	13	1	27	16	16	4
Liaison aircraft	0	0	8	0	0	0

Airborne division, TO&E 71, October 15, 1942, with Changes 1 & 2, 24 February 24, 1944

the lighter British airborne 6-pdr, which was substituted for the 37mm gun in Normandy. The divisions also attempted to improve their artillery firepower by substituting the M3 105mm howitzer for the 75mm pack howitzer in one field artillery battalion, which took place prior to the Normandy landings even though not officially authorized.

The August 1944 TO&E made very modest changes to the division, for example adding a parachute maintenance company. The first major reorganization occurred under the December 1944 table, in large measure due to the Army chief-of-staff Gen. George C. Marshall insisting that the airborne division commanders' views be taken into account. Gen. Maxwell Taylor of the 101st Airborne Division was flown to Washington specifically for this purpose, the reason he was not in command of the division when it was abruptly trucked to Bastogne on December 19, 1944, during the Battle of the Bulge. The December 1944 reorganization finally institutionalized the shift to two parachute infantry regiments and one glider infantry regiment, and a significant increase in equipment and personnel. It also codified practices that had already taken place, such as the addition of a third battalion to the glider infantry regiment. The division's various support elements were consolidated under divisional special troops, which included a military

QM co.	Signal co.	Medical co.	Anti-aircraft bn.	Ordnance co.	Medical/chaplain attachment	Total
5	5	21	28	8	42	564
86	95	195	476	69	263	8,032
0	0	0	0	0	84	2,403
1	1	0	2	1	0	101
82	99	0	502	76	0	4,803
0	0	0	0	0	0	3,066
0	4	0	0	0	0	152
8	0	0	0	0	0	92
0	0	0	0	0	0	179
0	0	0	0	0	0	16
5	4	0	0	5	0	445
4	0	0	36	0	0	109
0	0	0	0	0	0	75
0	0	0	0	0	0	36
0	0	0	24	0	0	44
0	0	0	0	0	0	36
0	0	0	42	0	0	233
0	0	0	0	0	0	20
4	0	4	15	2	0	205
0	0	0	0	0	0	2
30	4	23	44	15	23	323
0	0	2	0	0	0	17
0	0	0	2	6	0	85
30	4	20	44	15	20	215
0	0	0	2	5	0	100
0	0	0	0	0	0	8

police platoon, recon platoon, ordnance company, quartermaster company and signal company. The early tables had been much too austere in providing rear area administrative units, and the December 1944 tables attempted to rectify this situation by strengthening the support elements as well as the combat elements. The divisions in the ETO reorganized under this table in February–March 1945.

Even after the December 1944 additions, the airborne division still had problems. A postwar study of divisional organization by the General Board concluded:

The airborne division has worked under several handicaps which limited the missions to which it could be assigned with expectation of complete success. It has very little transportation and is in effect a foot division once on the ground. Its artillery is light and engineer construction equipment is practically nil. Higher headquarters have always had to attach many extra units to the airborne division in order that it might keep up with the others ... The results obtained by attaching extra troops to an airborne division were not as good as they would have been had these troops been organically part of the division.

Airborne division, TO&E 71, August 1, 1944

	HQ & HQ co.	Divisional artillery	Parachute infantry regiment	Glider infantry regt. (x2)	Anti-aircraft bn.	Engineer bn.
Officers	49	105	109	80	31	23
Enlisted men	141	1,243	1,859	1,474	458	374
.45-cal. pistol	20	255	11	9	3	3
.30-cal. carbine	160	57	1,093	1,098	814	438
.30-cal. M1 rifle	0	0	859	683	0	256
.30-cal. M1C rifle	0	0	27	12	0	0
.45-cal. SMG	0	0	54	36	48	18
.30-cal. BAR	0	0	0	36	0	0
.30-cal. LMG	0	0	132	12	0	11
.30-cal. HMG	0	0	0	8	0	0
2.36in. bazooka	10	173	73	81	0	25
.50-cal. HMG	3	37	4	3	36	0
60mm mortar	0	0	27	24	0	0
81mm mortar	0	0	12	12	0	0
37mm AT gun	0	0	0	8	0	0
37mm AA gun		0	0	0	24	0
75mm howitzer	0	40	0	0	0	0
Handcart	0	26	34	96	42	18
Motor scooter	4	50	52	29	15	25
1/4-ton jeep	9	111	15	21	44	18
3/4-ton truck	5	8	1	1	2	0
2 1/2-ton truck	10	27	15	10	2	5
1/4-ton trailer	12	79	15	13	44	8
1-ton trailer	10	27	15	10	2	4
Liaison aircraft	0	8	0	0	0	0

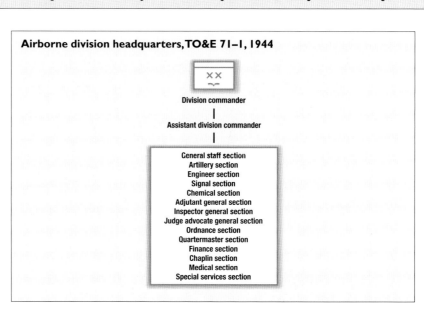

Airborne division headquarters, TO&E 71–1, 1944

Division commander

Assistant division commander

General staff section
Artillery section
Engineer section
Signal section
Chemical section
Adjutant general section
Inspector general section
Judge advocate general section
Ordnance section
Quartermaster section
Finance section
Chaplin section
Medical section
Special services section

Medical co.	Ordnance co.	QM prct. mnt. co.	QM co.	Signal co.	MP platoon	Medical/ chaplain attachment	Total
21	8	4	5	8	2	38	563
183	67	128	82	123	34	295	7,935
0	1	1	2	2	1	0	317
138	0	50	118	54	129	15	5,262
0	21	13	31	0	4	0	2,550
0	0	0	0	0	0	0	51
0	3	0	0	0	16	0	211
0	0	0	0	0	0	0	72
0	0	0	0	0	2	0	169
0	0	0	0	0	0	0	16
0	5	5	5	4	4	0	466
0	2	0	4	0	0	0	92
0	0	0	0	0	0	0	75
0	0	0	0	0	0	0	36
0	0	0	0	0	0	0	16
0	0	0	0	0	0	0	24
0	0	0	0	0	0	0	40
0	0	0	0	0	0	0	312
5	2	10	4	9	2	0	236
23	15	5	30	11	4	18	345
0	0	0	0	0	0	6	24
0	6	5	0	0	0	0	90
23	15	5	30	11	4	18	290
0	5	5	0	0	0	0	88
0	0	0	0	0	0	0	8

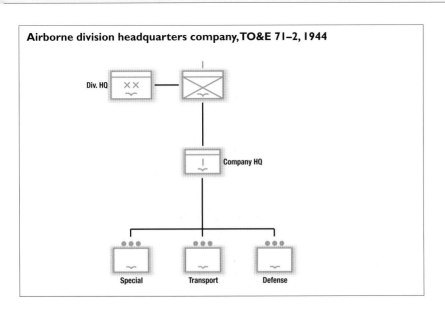

Airborne division headquarters company, TO&E 71–2, 1944

Div. HQ ××

Company HQ

Special   Transport   Defense

Airborne division, TO&E 71T, December 16, 1944

	Division HQ	Special troops	Parachute infantry regt. (x2)	Glider infantry regt.	Divisional artillery
Officers	63	58	136	140	146
Enlisted men	107	965	2,228	2,838	1,831
.45-cal. pistol	26	36	11	293	405
.30-cal. carbine	134	677	484	761	1,572
.30-cal. M1 rifle	0	247	1,809	1,816	
.30-cal. M1C rifle	0	0	27	27	0
.45-cal. SMG	0	110	54	63	12
.30-cal. BAR	0	3	81	135	0
.30-cal. LMG	0	2	105	36	0
.30-cal. HMG	0	0	0	24	0
2.36in. bazooka	0	37	73	108	240
.50-cal. HMG	0	36	8	23	54
60mm mortar	0	0	27	27	0
81mm mortar	0	0	12	18	0
57mm AT gun	0	0	0	18	8
75mm howitzer	0	0	0	0	60
Handcart	0	0	34	0	36
Motorcycle	0	33	52		62
1/4-ton jeep	0	176	24	187	196
3/4-ton truck	0	9	0	11	9
1 1/2-ton truck	0	5	0	1	0
2 1/2-ton truck	0	85	30	29	42
1/4-ton trailer	0	119	24	107	149
1-ton trailer	0	88	30	19	42
Liaison aircraft	0	0	0	0	10

Comparison of airborne division tables 1944	Feb 24, 44	Aug 1, 44	Dec 16, 44
Officers	564	563	824
Enlisted men	8,032	7,935	12,211
.45-cal. pistol	101	317	789
.30-cal. carbine	4,803	5,262	5,037
.30-cal. M1 rifle	3,066	2,550	6,049
.30-cal. M1C rifle	0	51	81
.45-cal. SMG	152	211	383
.30-cal. BAR	92	72	300
.30-cal. LMG	179	169	260
.30-cal. HMG	16	16	24
2.36in. bazooka	445	466	567

(continues on page 25)

Anti-aircraft bn.	Engineer bn.	Medical co.	QM prct. mnt. co.	Medical/chaplain attachment	Total
37	25	27	6	50	824
604	467	273	233	437	12,211
3	3	0	1	0	789
566	138	0	221	0	5,037
0	351	0	17	0	6,049
0	0	0	0	0	81
72	18	0	0	0	383
0	0	0	0	0	300
0	12	0	0	0	260
0	0	0	0	0	24
0	31	0	5	0	567
36	0	0	0	0	165
0	0	0	0	0	81
0	0	0	0	0	42
24	0	0	0	0	50
0	0	0	0	0	60
60	21	0	0	0	185
15	25	5	16	0	260
68	20	23	5	27	750
2	0	0	0	4	35
0	0	0	0	0	6
2	8	2	6	3	237
44	8	23	5	28	531
2	8	0	5	2	226
0	0	0	0	0	10

.50-cal. HMG	109	92	165
60mm mortar	75	75	81
81mm mortar	36	36	42
AT gun	44	16	50
75mm howitzer	36	40	60
Handcart	253	312	185
Motorcycle	207	236	260
1/4-ton jeep	323	345	750
3/4-ton truck	17	24	35
1 1/2-ton truck	0	0	6
2 1/2-ton truck	85	90	237
1/4-ton trailer	215	290	531
1-ton trailer	100	88	226
Liaison aircraft	8	8	10

As Gen. Maxwell Taylor pointed out after the war, of the 192 days spent in combat by the 101st Airborne Division, only four days were spent as an isolated airborne formation while the remaining 188 days of combat were spent as a conventional ground division as part of a larger Allied formation.

Parachute infantry regiment

The parachute infantry regiment (PIR) was the oldest of the airborne formations, pre-dating the airborne division. The first table of organization was authorized on February 17, 1942, and underwent three changes prior to D-Day: in July 1942, October 1943 and February 1944. Most of these were fairly modest, for example deleting the M1903 Springfield .30-cal. sniper rifle, and adding the 2.36in. bazooka anti-tank rocket launcher. The first large changes occurred under the December 1944 TO&E, with the PIR receiving additional troops and equipment. The most noticeable change was the increase in strength in the parachute infantry battalions due to the addition of a third rifle squad in each rifle platoon; previously there had only been two. Even after the expansion, this formation was only about two-thirds the size of a conventional infantry regiment. This was in part due to an absence of some of the supporting arms, for example the lack of the cannon company and anti-tank company found in a conventional infantry regiment. In addition, the organizational structure and logistical support was far more austere: 16 versus 34 2½-ton trucks; one versus four 1¾- and 1½-ton trucks; 15 versus 149 jeeps. Furthermore, the discrepancy was even greater when comparing the number of vehicles actually deployed in combat, since, in the case of the parachute regiment, only a portion of the jeeps were delivered if there was enough space in the gliders and no heavier trucks were airlifted.

The parachute infantry regiment's basic tactical unit was the parachute infantry battalion. The structure of the battalion changed little until the December 1944 tentative table, which added an additional rifle squad to each rifle platoon, thereby considerably increasing the overall strength of the battalion. The battalion's basic tactical unit was the rifle company, which consisted of a company headquarters and three rifle platoons. The rifle platoon organization under the February 1944 table was a platoon HQ, two rifle squads, and a 60mm mortar squad; the December 1944 table added a third rifle squad increasing the platoon strength from 36 to 49. The platoon headquarters was

A paratrooper of the 101st Airborne Division prepares his gear at an airfield in England on the night of June 5, prior to the Operation *Neptune* jump in Normandy. (NARA)

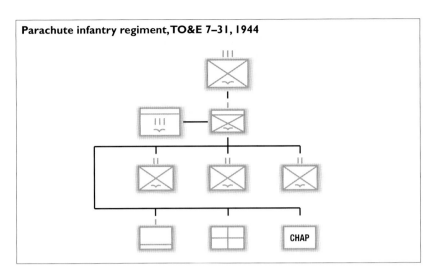

Parachute infantry regiment, TO&E 7–31, 1944

Parachute infantry regiment, TO&E 7–3, February 17, 1942; Changes 1, 2 & 3—February, 24 1944					
	HQ and HQ co.	**Service co.**	**Battalion (x3)**	**Attached medical/chaplain**	**Total**
Officers	13	13	35	11	142
Enlisted men	139	194	495	60	1,878
Parachute	125	109	505	71	1,820
.45-cal. pistol	4	0	2	0	10
.30-cal. carbine	135	72	170	0	717
.30-cal. rifle	15	138	358	0	1,227
.45-cal. SMG	0	0	18	0	54
.30-cal. LMG	0	0	44	0	132
.50-cal. HMG	0	4	0	0	4
2.36in. bazooka	5	5	21	0	73
60mm mortar	0	0	9	0	27
81mm mortar	0	0	4	0	12
Handcart	0	27	0	0	27
Motor scooter	14	2	12	0	52
1/4-ton jeep	0	15	0	0	15
3/4-ton ambulance	0	2	0	0	2
3/4-ton truck	0	1	0	0	1
2 1/2-ton truck	0	16	0	0	16
1/4-ton trailer	0	10	0	0	10
1-ton trailer	0	16	0	0	16

led by a 1st lieutenant, with an assistant 2nd lieutenant added under the December 1944 table. The HQ also included five enlisted men, consisting of the platoon sergeant, a platoon guide sergeant, two messengers and a radioman equipped with an SCR-536 handy-talkie; support weapons included a bazooka and a sniper rifle. The rifle squads consisted of 12 enlisted men led by two sergeants: a squad leader and an assistant squad leader/demolitions specialist. The squad had seven riflemen plus a three-man machine-gun team armed with the .30-cal. Browning light machine gun consisting of a gunner, assistant

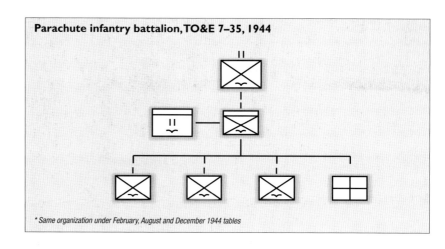

Parachute infantry battalion, TO&E 7–35, 1944

Same organization under February, August and December 1944 tables

Parachute infantry regiment, TO&E 7–31T, December 16, 1944

	HQ and HQ co.	Service co.	Battalion (x3)	Attached medical/chaplain	Total
Officers	16	9	37	11	147
Enlisted men	116	105	669	107	2,335
Parachute	159	140	847	0	2,810
.45-cal. pistol	5	0	2	0	11
.30-cal. carbine	31	9	148	0	484
.30-cal. M1 rifle	96	105	556	0	1,869
.30-cal. M1C rifle	0	0	9	0	27
.30-cal. BAR	0	0	27	0	81
.45-cal. SMG	0	0	18	0	54
.30-cal. LMG	0	0	35	0	105
.50-cal. HMG	0	8	0	0	8
2.36in. bazooka	5	5	21	0	73
60mm mortar	0	0	9	0	27
81mm mortar	0	0	4	0	12
Handcart	4	6	8	0	34
Motorcycle	0	52	0	0	52
1/4-ton jeep	0	24	0	4	28
3/4-ton ambulance	0	0	0	2	2
2 1/2-ton truck	0	30	0	1	31
1/4-ton trailer	0	24	0	4	28
1-ton trailer	0	30	0	1	31

gunner and ammo bearer with up to two light machine guns. All members of the rifle squad were armed with .30-cal. M1 Garand rifles except for the machine-gun team, who were armed with .30-cal. carbines. The December 1944 table substituted a .30-cal. BAR (Browning automatic rifle) for one of the .30-cal. light machine guns. Although the same size as a regular infantry company's rifle squad, the parachute rifle squad had more firepower with two .30-cal. machine guns/BARs versus one BAR in the regular squad. The mortar squad included six enlisted men led by a squad sergeant, a mortar gunner, an assistant gunner and three ammo bearers. The mortar squad's primary weapon was a 60mm M2 mortar and all squad members were armed with a .30-cal.

A stick of paratroopers of the 1/501st PIR wait for the green light inside a C-47 over the Netherlands during Operation *Market* in September 1944. (NARA)

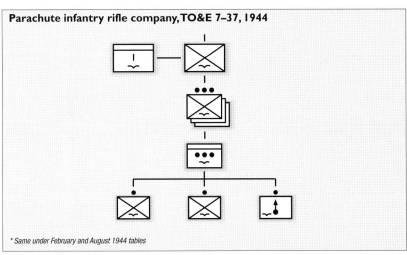

Parachute infantry rifle company, TO&E 7–37, 1944

* Same under February and August 1944 tables

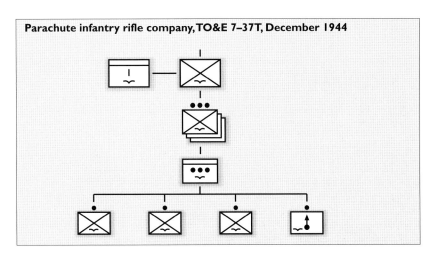

Parachute infantry rifle company, TO&E 7–37T, December 1944

carbine. It should be noted that paratrooper armament was heavier than the tables suggest. Although the tables did not authorize paratroopers to carry additional weapons such as a pistol, in practice many paratroopers obtained pistols almost as a matter of routine. Indeed, the postwar General Board study recommended that a secondary pistol armament become a standard equipment authorization based on the wartime experience.

Parachute infantry battalion, TO&E 7–35, 1944, February 17, 1942, Changes 1 & 2—February 24, 1944

	HQ & HQ co.	Rifle company (x3)	Attached medical	Total
Officers	11	8	2	37
Enlisted men	138	119	17	512
Parachute	124	127	19	524
.45-cal. pistol	2	0	0	2
.30-cal. carbine	107	21	0	170
.30-cal. rifle	40	106	0	358
.45-cal. SMG	0	6	0	18
.30-cal. LMG	8	12	0	44
2.36in. bazooka	9	4	0	21
60mm mortar	0	3	0	9
81mm mortar	4	0	0	4
Motor scooter	12	0	0	12

Parachute infantry battalion, TO&E 7–35T, December 16. 1944

	HQ & HQ co.	Rifle company (x3)	Attached medical	Total
Officers	13	8	2	38
Enlisted men	165	168	28	697
T-5 parachute	214	211	0	847
.45-cal. pistol	2	0	0	2
.30-cal. carbine	52	32	0	148
.30-cal. M1 rifle	124	144	0	556
.30-cal. M1C rifle	0	3	0	9
.30-cal. BAR	0	9	0	27
.45-cal. SMG	0	6	0	18
.30-cal. LMG	8	9	0	35
2.36in. bazooka	9	4	0	21
60mm mortar	0	3	0	9
81mm mortar	4	0	0	4
Handcart	8	0	0	8

Rifle squad, parachute infantry platoon, TO&E 3–37T, December 1944

Legend
a Squad Leader
b Assistant Squad Leader (demolitions)
c MG Gunner
d Assistant MG Gunner
e Ammo Bearer
f Rifleman
g Rifleman (grenadier)

a b c d e f g f f f f f

Artillery support in the airborne regiments was weak, so the four 81mm mortars found in each battalion's headquarters company were especially vital for fire support. This 81mm mortar from the 101st Airborne Division is seen in action on January 31, 1945, towards the end of the Ardennes campaign. (NARA)

Rifle squad, glider infantry platoon, TO&E 7–57T, December 1944

a	b	c	d	e	f	f	g	g	g	g	g

Legend
a   Squad Leader
b   Assistant Squad Leader
c   Auto Rifleman
d   Assistant Auto Rifleman
e   Ammo Bearer
f   Rifleman (grenadier)
g   Rifleman

* Aside from NCO's, the oother ten enlisted men in squad could include ranks of Technician grade 4, Technician grade 3, Private first class, or Private

Glider infantry regiment

The glider infantry regiment's basic tactical unit was the glider infantry battalion. As in the case of other airborne units, the regiment expanded under the December 1944 TO&E, primarily due to the addition of a third glider infantry battalion and the addition of a third rifle platoon in each company, bringing it more in line with parachute infantry and conventional infantry organization. The glider infantry battalion was organized somewhat differently from the parachute infantry battalion since the added airlift capability permitted the unit to bring in heavier weapons than was the case with the parachute battalion. So besides the three rifle companies, each battalion also deployed a jeep-borne heavy weapons company, which included eight .30-cal heavy machine guns and six 81mm mortars; the HQ company had an anti-tank platoon with three towed 57mm anti-tank guns. The use of gliders also permitted the battalion to bring in more vehicles, totaling 44 jeeps.

Anti-tank weapons were limited in the airborne division and the 2.36in. bazooka was the backbone of anti-tank defense. This team from the 325th GIR, 82nd Airborne Division, is seen covering a road in Belgium on December 20, 1944, during the division's efforts to halt the advance of the 1st SS-Panzer Division. (NARA)

The glider infantry company also had a different organization from its parachute counterpart, having a weapons platoon and two rifle platoons versus three parachute rifle platoons under the February 1944 tables. The weapons platoon had two .30-cal. heavy machine guns and two 60mm mortars. The glider company increased under the December 1944 tables when a third rifle platoon was added, making them larger than the parachute infantry companies. This organizational difference also affected the glider platoons and squads since the heavy weapons were concentrated in the glider company's weapons platoons instead of being spread out as in the parachute platoons. So the glider platoons initially consisted of three rifle squads, with 12 riflemen per squad all equipped with .30-cal. rifles. The December 1944 reorganization changed this, adding a BAR to the rifle squads and thereby bringing them closer to regular infantry squad organization.

Gliders were the only method of delivering heavier equipment such as jeeps. This is a medical jeep of the 327th GIR being loaded aboard of CG-4A of the 434th Troop Carrier Group on September 17, 1944, part of the two glider serials conducted on the first day of Operation *Market* from Aldermaston. The prong fitted on the glider nose is a Griswold reinforcement added to the nose of CG-4A gliders to give the crew added protection. (NARA)

The water-cooled M1917A1 .30-cal. heavy machine gun was not commonly found in the airborne division, but was used by the machine-gun platoon of the headquarters company in each glider infantry battalion. This example is in use by a team from the 82nd Airborne Division in Normandy after D-Day. (MHI)

Glider infantry regiment, TO&E 7–51, September 15, 1942; Changes 1 & 2—February 24, 1944					
	HQ and HQ co.	Service co.	Battalion (x2)	Attached medical/chaplain	Total
Officers	17	7	23	9	76
Enlisted men	217	79	621	64	1,602
.45-cal. pistol	3	1	2	0	8
.30-cal. carbine	165	25	268	0	766
.30-cal. rifle	66	54	336	0	792
.30-cal. BAR	0	6	18	0	42
.45-cal. SMG	0	0	18	0	36
.30 cal LMG	0	0	4	0	8
.30-cal. HMG	0	0	6	0	12
.50-cal. HMG	0	0	3	0	3
2.36in. bazooka	7	10	28	0	73
60mm mortar	0	0	12	0	12
81mm mortar	0	0	6	0	6
37mm AT gun	0	8	0	0	8
Handcart	16	0	28	0	72
Motor scooter	29	0	0	0	29
1/4-ton jeep	0	20	0	5	25
3/4-ton truck	0	1	0	0	1
2 1/2-ton truck	0	10	0	0	10
1/4-ton trailer	0	12	0	5	17
1-ton trailer	0	10	0	0	10

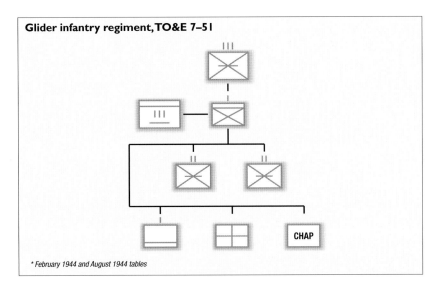

Glider infantry regiment, TO&E 7–51

* February 1944 and August 1944 tables

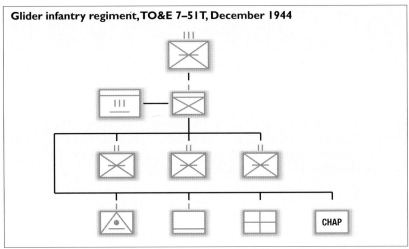

Glider infantry regiment, TO&E 7–51T, December 1944

This CG-4A from Serial A-47 of the 434th Troop Carrier Group has lost much of the fabric from its nose after having landed at Landing Zone W during Operation *Market*. The CG-4A had a special mechanism for quickly opening the nose to disembark its jeep cargo. (NARA)

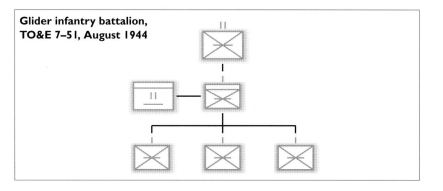

**Glider infantry battalion,
TO&E 7–51, August 1944**

Glider infantry regiment, TO&E 7–51T, December 16, 1944

	HQ and HQ co.	Service co.	Anti-tank battery	Battalion (x3)	Attached medical/chaplain	Total
Officers	13	15	7	35	13	153
Enlisted men	91	100	163	828	123	2,961
.45-cal. pistol	4	1	45	81	0	293
.30-cal. carbine	24	32	48	219	0	761
.30-cal. M1 rifle	76	82	77	527	0	1,816
.30-cal. M1C rifle	0	0	0	9	0	27
.30-cal. BAR	0	0	0	45	0	293
.45-cal. SMG	3	0	0	20	0	63
.30-cal. LMG	0	0	0	12	0	36
.30-cal. HMG	0	0	0	8	0	24
.50-cal. HMG	2	8	1	4	0	23
2.36in. bazooka	4	8	9	29	0	108
60mm mortar	0	0	0	9	0	27
81mm mortar	0	0	0	6	0	18
57mm AT gun	0	0	9	3	0	18
1/4-ton jeep	19	6	30	44	10	197
3/4-ton truck	1	2	2	2	0	11
1 1/2-ton truck	0	0	1	0	0	1
2 1/2-ton truck	1	28	0	0	1	30
1/4-ton trailer	0	0	0	9	0	27
1-ton trailer	4	0	16	29	10	117

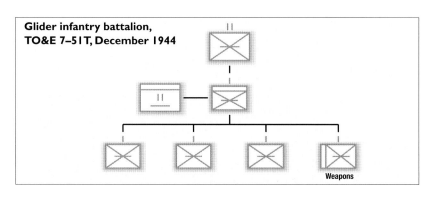

**Glider infantry battalion,
TO&E 7–51T, December 1944**

Weapons

The Horsa glider was not as popular in US glider units as the smaller CG-4A due to its higher maintenance demands and the vulnerability of its plywood construction to break-up on landing. Here, some glider infantry of the 82nd Airborne Division look over a Horsa that landed on D-Day. (NARA)

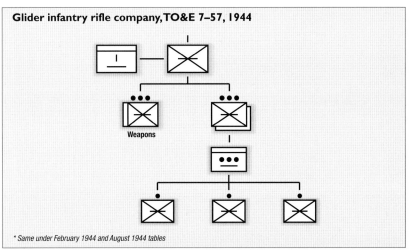

Glider infantry rifle company, TO&E 7–57, 1944

Weapons

* Same under February 1944 and August 1944 tables

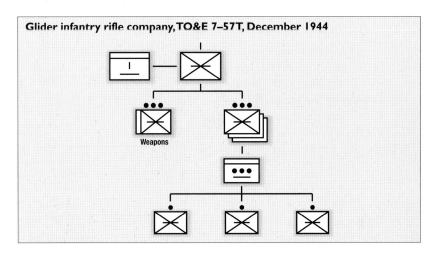

Glider infantry rifle company, TO&E 7–57T, December 1944

Weapons

Airborne artillery

Divisional artillery in an airborne division was significantly lighter than in infantry divisions due to the limitations of airlift. The February 1944 tables allotted three 75mm pack howitzer battalions, one parachute and two glider, compared to four battalions in an infantry division, three 105mm and one 155mm howitzer. The standard weapon in the airborne divisions was the 75mm pack howitzer, which was broken down into several loads for parachute delivery or which could be carried inside the CG-4A glider. It took nine paracrate loads to deliver a single pack howitzer by parachute: 1) rear trails; 2) rear trails; 3) gun sleigh; 4) gun cradle; 5) gun tube; 6) gun breech; 7) wheels; 8) ten rounds of ammunition; 9) para-caisson and six rounds of ammo. The parachute-dropped pack howitzer proved to be a liability in combat as, if there was any dispersion during the drop, the missing parts prevented the weapon from being assembled. The British attempted to circumvent this problem by developing a parachute pallet large enough for the pack howitzer to be dropped from a heavy bomber and these were used on D-Day in Normandy. However, the bomb bays on US bombers were not as well suited to this configuration as those on the British bombers, so US divisions in World War II did not use this method of delivery.

The M3 105mm howitzer had been designed specifically for airborne use but it was not authorized under the wartime tables until December 1944 and even then as an option. However, in practice the divisions began receiving an additional battalion equipped with this weapon in time for D-Day and, by 1945, the weapon was in service in all the airborne divisions in the ETO, using glider delivery.

There was some hope that the new recoilless rifles being developed in 1944 could solve the problems of airborne artillery. Fifty M18 57mm recoilless rifles were shipped to the ETO in March 1945 and could be air dropped using the M10 paracrate, which included the weapon and 14 rounds of ammunition. Some of these were delivered to the 17th Airborne Division and used in

A major problem facing the parachute field artillery was the need to break the 75mm M1A1 pack howitzer into several loads for parachute delivery. This created the risk that key elements would be lost during the airdrop. Here, gunners from the 101st Airborne Division re-assemble a 75mm pack howitzer following a practice jump near Newbury in England on November 23, 1943. (MHI)

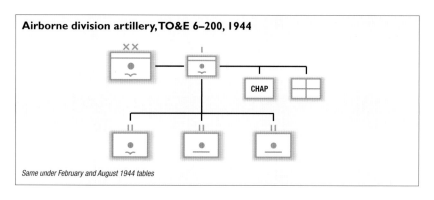

Airborne division artillery, TO&E 6–200, 1944

Same under February and August 1944 tables

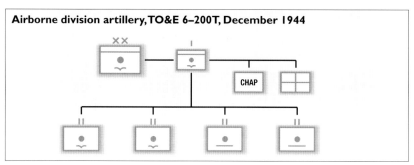

Airborne division artillery, TO&E 6–200T, December 1944

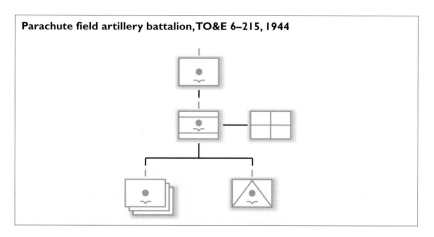

Parachute field artillery battalion, TO&E 6–215, 1944

There was some hope that innovations in artillery could help improve the airborne division's firepower. Recoilless rifles entered production too late to have a major effect, but a modest number of 57mm recoilless rifles were deployed with the 17th Airborne Division for Operation *Varsity* in March 1945 as seen here. (NARA)

Glider field artillery battalion, TO&E 6–225, 1944

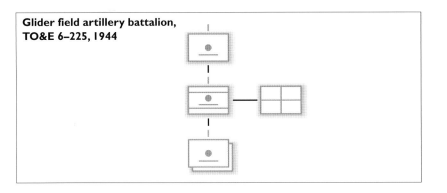

Parachute field artillery battalion, TO&E 6–215, September 5, 1942; Change 1—February 24, 1944

	HQ & service battery	75mm battery (x3)	AT & AA battery	Attached medical	Total
Officers	21	4	6	2	39
Enlisted men	163	90	88	13	534
.45-cal. pistol	10	0	0	0	10
.30-cal. carbine	172	94	94	0	548
.50-cal. HMG	4	4	8	0	24
2.36in. bazooka	14	14	14	0	70
37mm AT gun	0	0	4	0	4
75mm pack howitzer	0	4	0	0	12
Handcart	2	2	4	0	12
1/4-ton jeep	15	0	6	2	23
2 1/2-ton truck	18	0	0	0	18
1/4-ton trailer	0	0	2	1	3
1-ton trailer	18	0	0	0	18

Glider field artillery battalion, TO&E 6–225, September 5, 1942; Change 1—February 24, 1944

	HQ & service battery	75mm battery (x2)	Attached medical	Total
Officers	15	4	2	25
Enlisted men	94	133	11	371
.45-cal. pistol	12	0	0	12
.30-cal. carbine	97	137	0	371
.50-cal. HMG	3	6	0	15
2.36in. bazooka	14	18	0	50
37mm AT gun	0	0	0	0
75mm pack howitzer	0	6	0	12
Handcart	2	0	0	2
Motor scooter	9	4	0	17
1/4-ton jeep	5	16	2	39
3/4-ton truck	1	1	0	3
2 1/2-ton truck	4	0	0	4
1/4-ton trailer	5	3	1	11
1-ton trailer	4	0	0	4
Liaison aircraft	2	0	0	2

Operation *Varsity*. The 57mm recoilless rifle was not powerful enough to substitute for the 75mm pack howitzer, and instead was used as an infantry heavy weapon for direct support, bridging the gap between the 2.36in. bazooka and the pack howitzer. A more effective artillery weapon was the M20 75mm recoilless rifle, which was also shipped to the ETO in small numbers shortly before Operation *Varsity*. This was a crew-served weapon mounted on a tripod. The 75mm recoilless rifle proved well suited as dual-role weapon suitable for either anti-tank or direct-fire missions. During the Operation *Varsity* air-landings, 75mm recoilless rifles with the 507th PIR accounted for at least three German armored vehicles. Larger recoilless rifles were also under development but were not fielded prior to the end of the war.

Airborne engineer battalion

The airborne engineer battalion was unusual in that it was a mixed parachute/glider formation with two of its companies configured for glider delivery and one for parachute delivery, reflecting its usual deployment on the basis of one company per parachute/glider infantry regiment. The battalion was the usual "jack-of-all-trades," typical of engineer formations, but with a stronger emphasis on demolition work due to the nature of airborne missions. The engineer battalion was also responsible for some limited construction tasks, and was authorized a special lightweight dozer and grader that could be delivered by glider. There had been some consideration to developing a divisional capability for creating improvised runway improvement/construction to assist in follow-on air-landing missions, but this mission was usually pushed off on the AAF engineers who already specialized in these tasks.

Airborne engineer battalion, TO&E 5–225, September 5, 1942; Change 1– February 24, 1944					
	Battalion HQ & HQ/svc. co.	Parachute co.	Glider co. (x2)	Attached medical	Total
Officers	10	8	4	2	26
Enlisted Men	72	131	99	11	412
.45-cal. pistol	2	0	0	0	2
.30-cal. carbine	80	28	31	0	170
.30-cal. rifle	0	111	72	0	255
.45-cal. SMG	0	6	6	0	18
.30-cal. LMG	0	9	6	0	21
2.36in. bazooka	4	9	6	0	25
Flamethrower	0	3	0	0	3
Motor scooter	0	0	10	0	20
1/4-ton jeep	13	0	3	1	20
2 1/2-ton dump truck	4	0	0	0	4
DBHP crawler tractor	4	0	0	0	4
M3A4 handcart	5	5	5	0	20
1/4-ton trailer	2	0	3	1	9
1/2-ton dump trailer	10	0	0	0	10
1-ton trailer	4	0	0	0	4
Mine detector	5	5	5	0	20
Air compressor	2	0	0	0	2
6-ton pneumatic float	4	0	0	0	4
Recon boat	0	3	0	0	3

Airborne anti-aircraft battalion

Although called an anti-aircraft battalion, this unit was in fact a heavy weapons unit with three batteries of air-defense machine guns and three batteries of anti-tank guns. The air defense capability was generally not a high priority due to Allied air superiority, though the .50-cal. heavy machine guns could be used for general support. In the event of limitations on airlift, preference went to the battalion's anti-tank weapons and these battalions were seldom deployed in full strength. The battalion's anti-aircraft weapons were primarily the .50-cal. heavy machine gun, though under the August 1944 table the battalion was allotted the larger 37mm automatic cannon. However, this was removed under the final December 1944 table as the weapon was heavy, difficult to deliver and largely unnecessary. As mentioned earlier, the 1944 tables authorized the 37mm anti-tank gun, but the British 6-pdr was substituted in the 82nd and 101st Airborne Divisions prior to the Normandy landings. These weapons proved very useful in stemming several German armored attacks in Normandy so, by the time of the December 1944 tables, the 57mm gun had become officially accepted in spite of the need for glider delivery. The postwar General Board study concluded that this unit was unnecessary and its tasks better handled by artillery units since the new recoilless rifles were suitable for the anti-tank role.

The standard anti-aircraft weapon in the airborne divisions was the pedestal-mounted .50-cal. heavy machine gun, and an example is seen here near Wesel in March 1945 being used for perimeter security due to the lack of a significant air threat. (MHI)

The airborne division had relatively weak anti-tank capabilities, relying on bazookas and small numbers of 6-pdr (57mm) anti-tank guns. Nevertheless, these proved adequate to beat off an armored attack by the 17th SS-Panzergrenadier Division near Carentan as seen here with a knocked-out StuG IV assault gun behind a 6-pdr of the 82nd Airborne Division on June 13, 1944. (NARA)

Airborne anti-aircraft battalion, TO&E 4–275, 1944

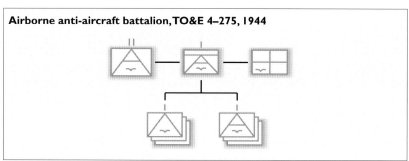

Airborne anti-aircraft battalion, TO&E 4–275, September 5, 1942; Change 1—February 24, 1944

	Battalion HQ	Auto weapons battery (x3)	MG battery (x3)	Attached medical	Total
Officers	7	3	4	2	30
Enlisted men	32	72	76	23	199
.45-cal. pistol	2	0	0	0	2
.30-cal. carbine	37	75	80	0	502
.50-cal. HMG	0	0	12	0	36
37mm anti-tank gun	0	8	0	0	24
M3A4 handcart	0	8	6	0	42
Motor scooter	3	2	2	0	15
1/4-ton jeep	2	8	6	2	46
3/4-ton truck	2	0	0	0	2
2 1/2-ton truck	2	0	0	0	2
1/4-ton trailer	2	8	6	2	46
1-ton trailer	2	0	0	0	2

Airborne tank battalion

The US Army considered forming special airborne tank units after the successful use of German paratroops at Eben Emael in 1940 and Crete in 1941, but lacked a suitable ultra-light tank. With the decision to proceed with the T9 airborne tank, in February 1943 the AGF ordered the Armored Force to organize an airborne tank battalion and develop suitable training and doctrine in cooperation with the Airborne Command. However, the Airborne Command was skeptical about the need for a battalion-sized formation due to the airlift problem, so the first unit was trimmed down to a company. The plan was to carry the tank under a C-54 transport, which would require air-landing since no large glider was available. The 151st Airborne Tank Company was activated at Ft. Knox on August 15, 1943, followed by the 28th Airborne Tank Battalion on December 6, 1943.

In spite of considerable enthusiasm within the army for the airborne tank concept, the Marmon Herrington T9E1 airborne tank proved to be so disappointing from a technical standpoint that enthusiasm soon waned. The 151st Airborne Tank Company was not available in time for deployment with

The lack of an airborne tank battalion led the 82nd Airborne Division to develop their own lightly armored version of the jeep for conducting reconnaissance and this patrol is seen in the Ardennes in December 1944. (NARA)

airborne units on D-Day, and in July 1944 was transferred from Ft. Knox to Camp Mackall, North Carolina, where it was quickly forgotten. The 28th Airborne Tank Battalion was reorganized as a conventional tank battalion in October 1944. The T9E1 airborne tank was finally accepted for service as the M22 airborne tank, and apparently a small number were sent to the 6th Army Group in 1944 in Alsace for potential use by the 1st Airborne Task Force. However, no airborne tank unit was deployed into combat during the war, in part due to a lack of a means to deliver them.

The British used airborne tanks on D-Day and again during Operation *Varsity* in 1945, delivering them with the enormous Hamilcar glider. However, the US Airborne Command never saw enough need for light tanks, so no Hamilcar gliders were requested from Britain. Curiously enough, the 17th Airborne Division did receive some support from M22 airborne tanks during Operation *Varsity*, but in British service with the 6th Airborne Armoured Reconnaissance Regiment.

Airborne tank battalion, TO&E 17–55, January 15, 1944					
	HQ & HQ company	Tank co. (x3)	Enlisted cadre	Medical detachment	Total
Officers	11	5	0	1	27
Enlisted men	128	72	109	12	465
.45-cal. pistol	3	0	0	0	3
.45-cal. SMG	40	57	0	0	211
.30-cal. carbine	84	20	0	0	144
.30-cal. LMG	16	2	0	0	22
.50-cal. M2 HMG	17	2	0	0	23
2.36in. bazooka	5	1	0	0	8
M22 airborne tank	2	18	0	0	56
75mm pack howitzer	3	0	0	0	3
1/4-ton jeep	26	4	0	3	41
3/4-ton WC truck	10	1	0	0	13
1/4-ton trailer	17	4	0	3	32

Airborne weapons and equipment

In general, the weapons used by the airborne divisions were the same as those in other US Army divisions, though a few weapons were developed specifically for the airborne. The standard M1 .30-cal. carbine was modified with a folding stock for airborne use to make it more compact. This became the standard sidearm in the airborne divisions, though it was unpopular in combat units due to its reliance on .30-cal. pistol ammunition, which was deemed to have insufficient range and stopping power. The other infantry weapons used by the airborne were the same as those issued to other infantry units though, as mentioned below, the tables of equipment differed. The paratroops did have some accessories for their small arms used when parachuting. The Griswold bag was designed to carry an M1 .30-cal. rifle disassembled into two parts during the jump, but some paratroopers preferred to jump with the rifle assembled and ready for use in spite of the potential landing hazard. A number of other weapons bags were developed for the jump, some of which were attached by a cord and lowered prior to landing to reduce the probability of injury. The one weapon found more commonly in paratrooper units than in other infantry formations was some form of knife, typically an M3 fighting knife or M2 switchblade. This was necessary to cut parachute lines in the event that the paratrooper landed in a tree, but paratroopers were also trained to use the knife as a weapon, especially for silent night attacks.

There was a significant concern about the threat posed by armored vehicles to the lightly armed airborne formations. Aside from the bazooka, a number of other weapons were issued to airborne troops to deal with this threat. The British No. 82 Gammon grenade was a small cloth bag filled with a 1kg charge of plastic explosive with an attached safeing and arming device. It was designed to be thrown against enemy armored vehicles, with the charge causing spall on the inside face of the Panzer's armor plate to injure the crew. It was difficult and dangerous to use effectively, but there are recorded cases of paratroopers knocking out German armored vehicles with them. Another last-ditch anti-tank weapon was the British Hawkins ATK 75 Mk. III anti-tank mine, which was a small rectangular mine powerful enough to blow off a tank track.

Besides the individual weapons, paratroopers had several specialized items of battledress and personal equipment. The paratrooper's M2 helmet was essentially similar to the standard infantry M1 helmet but, instead of the usual helmet strap, it had a more elaborate inverse A strap culminating in a leather chin strap. An improved paratrooper helmet, the M1C, entered development in October 1943 with a modified chin-strap suspension, but didn't become available until after the Normandy drops. Glider infantry wore the standard infantry helmet. Paratroopers were also issued brown-leather high-lace "jump" boots instead of the standard infantry boots; glider infantry received standard infantry boots. The paratroopers' M1942 battledress was distinct from that of the regular infantry due to a larger number of pockets, resulting in their legendary nickname "the devils in the baggy pants." When the new green M1943 battledress was issued after Normandy, there was no distinct paratrooper version though some units did modify their clothing with additional pockets.

The standard parachute used in 1944 was the T-5, which consisted of a main pack worn on the back with an associated harness. They were delivered either with a camouflaged or white canopy. Although there were efforts made to use only the camouflaged canopy during the Normandy night drop, in fact white canopies were also used. Unlike German and British paratroopers, US paratroopers also were issued an associated reserve AN 6513-1A chest pack, though it was of dubious utility in view of the low altitude at which most combat jumps were conducted. The T-5's most serious shortcoming was the lack of a quick-release on the harness, which was very dangerous if the paratrooper had the misfortune of landing in water as it was difficult and time-consuming to escape the harness. Due to the number of paratroopers drowned after landing in flooded areas in Normandy, divisional riggers modified the T-5's harnesses to incorporate a quick-release mechanism derived from the British design. The improved T-7 parachute with a quick-release mechanism was introduced before the end of the war. Besides the individual parachutes, heavier equipment was air dropped using the A-5 parapack container. This was a padded canvas bag with a parachute attached at one end. The parachute was color coded depending on the contents: blue for food rations, green for fuel, red or yellow for ammunition and explosives, and white for medical or signals equipment. For night drops, a small battery-powered lamp was attached which was color coded by attaching clear plastic covers over the bulbs on either end. The parapack was delivered either by pushing it out of the door of the transport aircraft, or suspended under the belly of the C-47 using a "para-rack," which shielded the container from the airstream and contained the necessary release clips.

Troop carrier organization

At the time of the D-Day landings, the AAF element of the airborne force was IX Troop Carrier Command, part of the Ninth Air Force, under the command of Brig. Gen. Paul Williams. This command consisted of three troop carrier wings with 14 troop carrier groups, and five groups per wing; the 50th TCW, which was the last to arrive, only had four groups. In addition, there was the Provisional Pathfinder Group, directly under IX TCC headquarters, which would be responsible for delivering the airborne pathfinder teams in advance of the main airdrop. Each group typically was allotted four squadrons with a nominal strength of 64 operational aircraft and 16 in reserve. Each squadron had a nominal strength of 12 aircraft plus one as an attrition spare. In total, IX TCC deployed 56 squadrons of C-47 and C-53 transport aircraft totaling some 1,022

The workhorse of the troop carrier units was the Douglas C-47 Skytrain. The antenna below the cockpit window is for the Rebecca homing system used for navigation to the drop zone. "Empress Mary Ellen" served with the 304th Troop Carrier Squadron, 442nd TCG, 50th TCW, and is seen here at Vertus, France, on February 26, 1945, with an ample array of paratroop, glider and supply missions marked on the side of the fuselage. (MHI)

aircraft and crew in June 1944. To foster better joint training, the troop carrier groups were paired with the divisions they would be lifting. So the 52nd Wing was assigned to the 82nd Airborne Division and the 53rd to the 101st Airborne.

The principal transport aircraft of the troop carrier squadrons was the Douglas C-47 Skytrain, a military derivative of the famous DC-3 airliner. The C-47 differed from its civilian counterpart in numerous details, but most noticeably in the spartan interior configuration and the provision of a large access door on the left rear fuselage, which could be employed for cargo handling as well as paratroop jumps. A portion of the force was equipped with the C-53, which was another militarized version of the DC-3 but without the enlarged cargo door. The other major cargo aircraft of the period, the C-46 Commando, was larger and faster than the C-47 but did not enter production in substantial numbers until 1943. It was not favored for the airborne delivery role due to its performance problems at the slow airdrop speeds. As a result, the C-47 was the principal airlift aircraft for US airborne operations in World War II. In 1945, the attitude towards the C-46 shifted due to the desire to be able to drop paratroopers more quickly than was possible from the C-47. The C-46 carried more paratroopers than the C-47 and had doors on either side for faster exit. As a result, a small number of C-46s were used on the final airborne mission of the war in the ETO, Operation *Varsity* in March 1945. However, they

The C-47 could be adapted to deliver para-packs using a special belly-mounted frame with fairings to protect the packs during flight. These troop carrier crews are seen installing this system on a C-47 at the airbase in Orléans, France, in March 1945 in preparation for Operation *Varsity*. (NARA)

More than 160 CG-4A assault gliders of the 434th Troop Carrier Group cover the field at Aldermaston on September 18, 1944, prior to the second day's glider missions to Landing Zone W in the Netherlands. (MHI)

were found to be more vulnerable to ground fire than the C-47, a flaw attributed to a hydraulic system that tended to leak inflammable fluid.

The principal assault glider in the troop carrier squadrons was the CG-4A, designed by Waco in 1942 to carry 15 fully armed infantrymen. Although the AAF also procured the smaller eight-to-nine seat CG-3A assault glider, it was later deemed too small for combat operations. Production of the CG-4A was authorized in August 1942 before development was complete due to the urgency of the requirement. However, the program was beset by production problems as the AAF limited the production contracts to companies not already heavily involved in aircraft production to avoid distracting the major aircraft manufacturers. As a result, production was scattered between 16 firms, mainly small aircraft firms, which had a great deal of trouble manufacturing these large gliders on schedule. Although intended as an inexpensive aircraft, the inexperience of many of the small firms led to serious cost escalation and the program was plagued as well by manufacturing problems leading to a string of accidents during flights in 1943. Although developed by Waco, the Ford Motor Company was the largest single CG-4A manufacturer and completed 2,418 of the 10,574 built through October 1944. Training flights with the CG-4A revealed that the nose section was very prone to damage. A number of solutions were proposed, and prior to Normandy, 288 CG-4A gliders were modified by installing Griswold reinforcements on the nose, which were a type of spider-shaped reinforcement designed to protect the crew during a hard landing. Other solutions to the problem included installing plywood reinforcing skids under the nose such as the single Parker skid or the triple Corey skid. Some gliders were also fitted with a rear-mounted drogue parachute deployed on landing to slow the glider and reduce the landing distance.

US troop transport and combat glider production in 1941–45						
	1941	1942	1943	1944	1945	Total
C-46	1	46	353	1,321	1,459	3,180
C-47	165	1,057	2,595	4,900	1,536	10,253
CG-4A	0	804	5,833	4,280	2,988	13,905
Other gliders	0	3	105	130	440	678

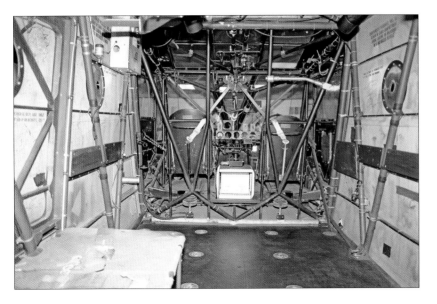

The CG-4A assault glider was constructed of tubular steel frames with a canvas covering as is evident from this interior view of the cockpit area of one of the few surviving examples, preserved at the airborne museum at Ft. Benning, Georgia. (Author's collection)

The delays in the manufacture of the CG-4A was one of the reasons that the US airborne divisions had a mix of two parachute and one glider regiments in 1943–44 in spite of the intended mix of two glider and one parachute regiments. Due to the production difficulties with the CG-4A in early 1943, the AAF approached Britain to see if there was any excess capacity in the manufacture of the larger Horsa assault glider. The Horsa was significantly larger than the CG-4A with seating for 28, but tests in 1943 concluded that it could be towed by the C-47. Prior to D-Day, IX TCC had received 360 Horsa gliders of which 301 were still operational. US acquisition of the Horsa was curtailed after the Normandy landing, as the air force complained that it demanded far too much maintenance compared to the CG-4A. The Horsa glider was thoroughly disliked by American glider pilots who felt that its plywood construction made it far more brittle than the CG-4A during landing, causing more wrecks and injuries. Although IX Troop Carrier Group still had 104 Horsa on hand in September 1944 at the time of Operation *Market*, the strong dislike of this type led to it being sidelined in favor of the exclusive use of the CG-4A.

Assault glider tow formations (single tow, double tow)

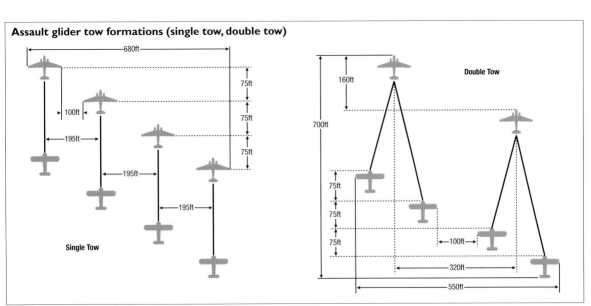

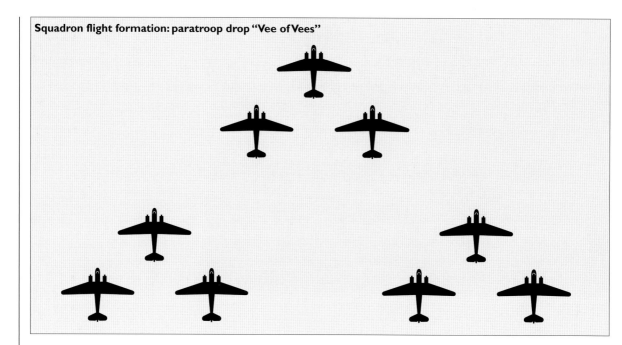

A larger 30-seat glider, the CG-13A, was also developed of which 81 were shipped to the ETO by the end of the war. However, none were used during Operation *Varsity* due to the added complexity its introduction would have entailed. An improved 15-seat glider was also developed to replace the CG-4A, and 87 CG-15A were shipped to the ETO, but too late to see use.

Although the Army Air Force had planned to recover and re-use gliders after operations, in the event this proved to be wishful thinking. A majority of the force was invariably damaged beyond repair after smashing into trees, walls and other obstructions, and even those landing in flat fields frequently suffered extensive damage. None of the 222 Horsa gliders used on D-Day were recovered, and only 15 of the 295 CG-4A gliders, a paltry 5 percent. After Operation *Market*, only 281 gliders were recovered of the 1,409 employed (14 percent) and the results were only slightly better after Operation *Varsity* with 148 of 908 CG-4A gliders recovered (16 percent). Furthermore, pilots were distrustful of the safety of these battered gliders and in reality none were ever re-used in combat.

The troop carrier groups had a nominal table of 104 glider pilots and prior to D-Day, IX Troop Carrier Command had 1,352 glider pilots and 445 glider co-pilots. After receiving some reinforcements, there were enough glider crews for 951 gliders on the eve of D-Day. A total of 2,100 CG-4A gliders were shipped to Britain by the time of D-Day. There had been some significant attrition due to training, mainly involving landing damage rather than total write-offs, so at the end of May 1944, there were 1,118 CG-4A gliders available.

During airdrop missions, the standard aircraft tactical formation was called a "serial," which was a formation of aircraft assigned to a specific drop zone (DZ) for paratroops or a landing zone (LZ) for gliders. Serials varied in number of aircraft; pathfinder serials were quite small, usually only three aircraft. The standard paratrooper serials were larger, typically 36–50 aircraft, or about four to six squadrons.

The distance between the tug and the glider complicated glider missions. Although the C-47 was capable of a double tug of two CG-4A gliders, this was hazardous at night and was not used until Operation *Varsity* in 1945. Some serials on D-Day were mixed paratrooper/glider missions; for example, when delivering paratrooper units with heavy equipment such as artillery and jeeps.

Doctrine called for glider pilots to be evacuated as soon as possible after the airborne landings as they were not regularly trained for ground combat. These glider pilots have been collected aboard an LCVP for transfer back to airbases in Britain following the D-Day landings in Normandy. (NARA)

Although each troop carrier squadron had 12 operational aircraft, the general practice was to employ nine per mission. This was linked to the standard formation of a "vee-of-vees" with each flight of three aircraft in a "V" formation and each of the three flights in turn forming a larger "V." The "vees" were staggered slightly upward behind the lead aircraft and the trailing "vees" upward of the lead "vees" to prevent paratroopers from hitting following aircraft when they jumped.

IX Troop Carrier Command Brig. Gen. Paul Williams	
1st Pathfinder Group (Prov)	1st PFS; 2nd PFS; 3rd PFS; 4th PFS
50th Troop Carrier Wing Brig. Gen. Julian Chappell	
439th Troop Carrier Group	91st TCS (L4)*; 92nd TCS (J8); 93rd TCS (3B); 94th TCS (D8)
440th Troop Carrier Group	95th TCS (9X); 96th TCS (6Z); 97th TCS (W6); 98th TCS (8Y)
441st Troop Carrier Group	99th TCS (3J); 100th TCS (8C); 301st TCS (Z4); 302nd TCS (2L)
442nd Troop Carrier Group	303rd TCS (J7); 304th TCS (V4); 305th TCS (4J); 306th TCS (7H)
52nd Troop Carrier Wing Brig. Gen. Harold Clark	
61st Troop Carrier Group	14th TCS (3I); 15th TCS (Y9); 53rd TCS (3A); 59th TCS (X5)
313th Troop Carrier Group	29th TCS (5X); 47th TCS (N3); 48th TCS (Z7); 49th TCS (H2)
314th Troop Carrier Group	32nd TCS (S2); 50th TCS (2R); 61st TCS (Q9); 62nd TCS (E5)
315th Troop Carrier Group	34th TCS (NM); 43rd TCS (UA); 309th TCS (M6); 310th TCS (4A)
316th Troop Carrier Group	36th TCS (6E); 36th TCS (W7); 44th TCS (4C); 45th TCS (T3)
53rd Troop Carrier Wing Brig. Gen. Maurice Beach	
434th Troop Carrier Group	71st TCS (CJ); 72nd TCS (CU); 73rd TCS (CN); 74th TCS (ID)
435th Troop Carrier Group	75th TCS (SH); 76th TCS (CW); 77th TCS (IB); 78th TCS (CM)
436th Troop Carrier Group	79th TCS (S6); 80th TCS (7D); 81st TCS (U5); 82nd TCS (3D)
437th Troop Carrier Group	83rd TCS (T2); 84th TCS (Z8); 85th TCS (9O); 86th TCS (5K)
438th Troop Carrier Group	87th TCS (3X); 88th TCS (M2); 89th TCS (4U); 90th TCS (Q7)

Alpha-numeric code after each squadron is the squadron code painted on the nose of the aircraft.

Within each serial, the paratroopers within each aircraft were called a "stick." The size of the sticks varied, usually 18–20 paratroopers per aircraft in most C-47 transports, but only nine to ten in parachute artillery units due to the amount of other equipment carried in the para-packs that were dropped with the stick. Likewise, the number of troops per glider varied depending on the combat load. The CG-4A glider had typical loads of two crew plus 13 glider infantry; or a jeep and four troops; or a 75mm howitzer, three troops and 18 rounds of ammunition. The Horsa glider had a standard load of two crewmen plus 28 glider infantry; or two jeeps and crew; or one 75mm pack howitzer plus jeep and crew.

Airborne tactics: the navigation problem

A critical technical and tactical problem faced in the early airborne operations was the difficulty of navigating transport aircraft at night to provide precision airborne delivery of the paratroopers and gliders. This was due to the relative immaturity of night navigation technology. The RAF had pioneered night navigation both for night bombing missions and the air delivery of supplies to resistance groups in France. The preferred British approach was to use Gee, a radio navigation system deployed in 1943 to assist RAF night bombing. Three British radio stations emitted a coded radio pulse that was monitored by the navigators on the transport aircraft who then used triangulation to determine their position on a map. The system was optimistically rated to have a margin of error of 1,200ft, though some experts believed it was closer to 2,000ft in range and 1,500ft in deflection. The system was vulnerable to German electronics jamming that could blind it for up to 15 miles from the jamming station. The first Gee set was mounted on a USAAF C-47 in January 1944 and, prior to D-Day, there were plans to fit 108 aircraft with the full set and 44 others with a partial set. The problem with adopting Gee was two fold: on the one hand there were not enough sets to go around; and, on the other hand, IX Troop Carrier Command was desperately short of navigators, with only about one for every three aircraft. In contrast, the smaller British transport force had a trained navigator for each aircraft.

As a result, IX Troop Carrier Command favored the Rebecca-Eureka system that had been used with some success in the Mediterranean. This system had originally been developed in Britain to assist in delivering supplies to the French resistance. The Rebecca was an airborne radio transponder that worked in conjunction with a ground-based Eureka radio beacon. The Rebecca activated the Eureka by coded radio pulses, and the Eureka beacon responded with the signals being acquired by Rebecca antennas on either side of the forward fuselage of the C-47. The signals helped the crew determine whether the drop zone was to the right or left. The US began manufacturing the Eureka Mk. IIIC in 1943 as the AN/PPN-2 beacon transmitter-receiver. The Eureka-Rebecca system was not particularly reliable at close range due to potential interference from the multiple

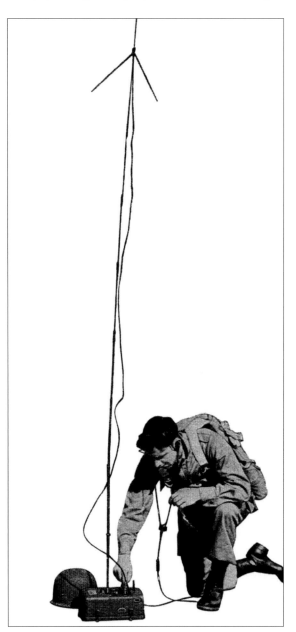

The key task of the pathfinders was the delivery of the Eureka beacon to the drop zone to serve as a navigation aid to the main airborne landings. This is the standard AN/PPS-2 version of the Eureka in the deployed configuration. (MHI)

beacons, so it had to be supplemented by some other device to inform the transport crew when they were over the drop zone. The method for night drops was the use of special holophane Aldis lights set up in a T pattern 30 yards long and 20 yards wide with the Eureka positioned 25 yards beyond the head of the T. To distinguish different drop zones, different colored lights were used.

The performance of the Eureka-Rebecca system depended on planting the Eureka and the associated lights accurately within the intended drop zone. This was the task of the pathfinders, an elite team in each airborne division delivered to the drop zone by special pathfinder squadrons from IX Troop Carrier Command.

Prior to the D-Day landings, a variety of improved navigational aids were being deployed. The new SCR-717 was an early form of ground-scanning radar and could help the navigator identify when the aircraft had passed over the coast due to the different radar reflectivity of water and ground; however, it was fairly useless over ground for navigation purposes due to backscatter. Shortly before D-Day, the BUPS responder beacon was developed which worked somewhat like Rebecca-Eureka in providing a blip on the radarscope when interrogated by the SCR-717 radar. Only about 50 SCR-717 radar sets were available at the time of the Normandy landings and flight leaders primarily used them, with the BUPS being planted along with Eureka.

These tactics for night drops had some serious weaknesses. The pathfinders could not be dropped too soon or their discovery would alert the Germans to an airborne attack; if dropped too late they would not have time to establish their beacons. As would become apparent during the D-Day missions, the pathfinders had considerable difficulty positioning their equipment in time. The accuracy of the drops was further undermined by the reliance on serial formation tactics due to the shortage of navigators. If the serial was disrupted by clouds or flak, the individual aircraft faced considerable difficulty in accurately locating the drop zone when lacking a navigator with the Gee navigation aid. The British approach was to use looser formations since all transport aircraft had a navigator and the Gee equipment, and so could navigate independently in the event they were scattered by weather or flak.

The navigation problems and resultant dispersion of the paratroopers during the D-Day drops severely compromised the ability of the 82nd and 101st Airborne Divisions to carry out their missions. The technical short-comings of the existing navigation technology convinced the First Allied Airborne Army to drop the idea of massed night drops. All major airborne drops after Operation *Neptune* were conducted in daylight. The presumption was that German flak positions could be suppressed by Allied airpower and that losses and disruption caused by flak would be less serious than problems induced by nighttime navigation issues.

Command and control

Command and control of the airborne forces can be considered at two levels, the operational and the tactical. At the tactical level, once the airborne force had landed and was involved in ground combat, command and control was essentially the same as with other US Army infantry formations except for the somewhat less extensive assortment of radios and other communication equipment. The more controversial issue was the operational command and control of airborne forces due to the need to coordinate the planning between the Army Ground Force elements and the Army Air Force elements. Although both the AGF and AAF were part of the US Army in World War II, they had separate chains of command and the AAF had a considerable amount of autonomy. The complicated story of the efforts to coordinate policy in the United States prior to the deployment to the ETO is outside the scope of this short book. This issue became even more complicated in 1943–44 when the US airborne divisions and troop carrier groups deployed to Britain since Eisenhower's Supreme Headquarters Allied Expeditionary Force (SHAEF) was committed to operational coordination between the US and British airborne forces, adding coordination with the British Army and RAF into the mix.

In June 1943, Air Chief Marshal Trafford Leigh-Mallory, chief of RAF Fighter Command, was appointed head of the tactical air forces assigned to Operation *Overlord*, the planned D-Day invasion. This command, the Allied Expeditionary Air Force (AEAF), was established in November 1943. In December 1943, the US Ninth Air Force was put under operational control of AEAF and Leigh-Mallory made it clear that he expected that airborne operations would be planned by his command in conjunction with Montgomery's 21st Army Group, which had operational control over the ground units assigned to *Overlord*. To facilitate this planning, an Airborne-Air Planning Committee was formed, chaired by Leigh-

Following the Normandy operation, Maj. Gen. Matthew Ridgway was appointed commander of XVIII Airborne Corps. This headquarters was frequently subordinated to Montgomery's 21st Army Group for operations, and the two commanders are seen here discussing missions during the Battle of the Bulge in December 1944. (MHI)

Mallory and including the US and British troop carrier commanders, airborne commanders and other key personnel. This organization established a Troop Carrier Command Post at Eastcote Place, which directed troop carrier operations for the invasion.

Although this organizational structure was instrumental in carrying out the airborne operations on D-Day, senior Allied ground commanders, especially Eisenhower, Montgomery and Bradley, made most of the critical tactical decisions. Leigh-Mallory's inexperience in airborne operations and his unduly pessimistic assessments of the chances of success of Allied airborne operations on D-Day led to his exclusion from actual decision making about the airborne operations. His failure to incorporate sufficient US officers into his new AEAF headquarters further weakened his influence and aggravated relations with Gen. Lewis Brereton's Ninth Air Force, so when Leigh-Mallory attempted to dictate IX Tactical Troop Command training policies, he was simply ignored. As a result of these leadership problems, AEAF failed to provide the basis for a unified Allied airborne command formation.

The obvious shortcomings of the AEAF even prior to the Normandy operation prompted the Airborne Sub-Section of the SHAEF G-3 (Operations) Division to recommend establishing a new Anglo-American airborne HQ. The early versions of this proposal envisioned leaving the troop carrier formations under AEAF control, but using the new command to conduct the airborne mission planning and assume operational control over the British and American airborne forces. Bradley's US First Army HQ accepted the need for some form of Allied airborne command to coordinate training, supply and airlift, but saw no need for unified control and preferred the establishment of

Commander of the 82nd Airborne Division, Maj. Gen. James Gavin, straps on his parachute at Cottesmore in preparation for Operation *Market* on September 17, 1944. (NARA)

Commander of the 101st Airborne Division, Maj. Gen. Maxwell Taylor, gives the photographer a smart salute after boarding a C-47 of the 435th Troop Carrier Group with the 1/502nd PIR at Welford on September 17, 1944. (NARA)

a US airborne corps instead to coordinate the growing US force. Eisenhower had a more visionary approach to the scheme, and wanted the new command to control not only the Anglo-American airborne force, but the airlift component as well, preferably under an air commander. Lt. Gen. F. A. M. Browning, commander of the British Airborne Troops, was not keen on this idea as there was some fear that it would establish a precedent for a later absorption of the British airborne force by the RAF. Eisenhower raised the issue with the US Army Chief of Staff, Gen. George C. Marshall, as well as the head of the AAF, Gen. "Hap" Arnold, who finally concurred.

Since the US was providing two-thirds of the airborne divisions and three-quarters of the troop carriers, on July 16, 1944, the new command was handed to a US officer, Gen. Lewis Brereton, commander of the Ninth Air Force that was currently in charge of IX Troop Carrier Command. Brereton was not entirely

Brig. Gen. Anthony McAuliffe (left) is better remembered for his command of the 101st Airborne Division at Bastogne, but was the division's artillery commander. He is seen here coordinating the defense of Veghel during Operation *Market* with Col. Sink (center) of the 506th PIR and Col. Harper (right) of the 327th GIR. (MHI)

convinced of the need for a combined airborne headquarters and he rightly pointed out that he expected that US ground commanders would not be too happy. In spite of this, the new organization made its debut on August 16, 1944, as the First Allied Airborne Army (FAAA), directly subordinate to SHAEF rather than to Montgomery's 21st Army Group or Bradley's 12th Army Group. Browning was the obvious choice as deputy commander to ensure that the command was indeed a joint effort both from the standpoint of army representation and British participation. Eisenhower's decision to appoint an air force commander was an astute political judgment, as it helped to ensure enthusiastic air force support of the future airborne missions, especially on the touchy subject of the diversion of heavy bombers for supplementary supply missions.

While the debate over a joint command was occurring, the ETOUSA (European Theater of Operations—US Army) was planning to establish a new command for the growing US airborne force in Europe. The commander of the 82nd Airborne Division, Gen. Matthew Ridgway, was the obvious choice due to his broad combat experience, and when the new XVIII Corps headquarters arrived in Europe in August 1944, it was re-designated as XVIII Airborne Corps. As a result of these developments, by the end of August, Brereton's new First Allied Airborne Army consisted of the US XVIII Airborne Corps, the British Airborne Troops, IX Troop Carrier Command and any RAF troop carrier formations allocated in the event of large-scale operations.

Controversy swirled around the new command in August, mostly coming from Bradley's 12th Army Group headquarters. Once Paris was captured, the Allied armies were outracing the supply of fuel and supplies, which had to rely on long road marches from the Normandy beaches since the Allied air forces had so thoroughly smashed up the French railroad system. Bradley wanted fuel airlifted to forward fields to assist the rapid advance. But IX Troop Carrier Command's primary mission was to deliver airborne troops, and there were a string of plans to conduct airborne missions through late July and August that led to some of the wings being sequestered and so not available for secondary supply missions. In addition, about a third of the command's strength was shipped south in early August to conduct the airborne drops associated with Operation *Dragoon* in southern France. Bradley accused the First Allied Airborne Army of withholding its resources for frivolous missions better performed by ground units and preferred the diversion of the troop carrier aircraft to vital transport assignments. This controversy became further embroiled in the bitter disagreements over whether priority for supplies should be allotted to Montgomery's 21st Army Group or Bradley's 12th Army Group in September 1944.

The later consensus about organization of the First Allied Airborne Army, free of the wartime antagonisms, was more positive. A postwar General Board study noted that:

> The organization of the First Allied Airborne Army, charged with the control and coordination of all phases of the airborne operations including planning, training, pre-invasion reconnaissance and bombing, troop carrier operations, escorts, anti-flak missions, and re-supply, was a concrete step forward. The merit in the unified command principle as applied to airborne operations was clearly demonstrated in its first test—the efficiently conducted daylight airborne assault on Holland.

The size limitations of the gliders forced the airborne to mount their command and control equipment on jeeps. This high-power SCR-499 radio has been mounted on a jeep with the accessories in the normal 1-ton trailer instead of the usual mounting in a shelter on the rear of a 2^1/$_2$-ton truck. (NARA)

Tactics

Operation *Neptune*: night drop over Normandy

The airborne landings that spearheaded the Operation *Neptune* amphibious assault on Normandy were the first US airborne operations employing a full division; previous missions were no larger than regimental combat teams. The mission of the 82nd and 101st Airborne Divisions changed considerably from the early conceptions in 1943 to the final plans in May 1944, gradually narrowing in focus to the mission of assisting the landings at Utah Beach. The February 1944 plan envisioned using the 101st Airborne Division immediately behind Utah Beach to secure the causeways off the beach that passed through areas flooded by the Germans to complicate access away from the landing areas. Bradley's First US Army planners wanted the more experienced 82nd Airborne Division dropped further west to permit a rapid cutoff of the Cotentin Peninsula, preventing the Germans from reinforcing Cherbourg, which was the main operational objective of the Utah landings. Only days before D-Day, Allied intelligence learned of the move of the German 91st Air-landing Division into the central Cotentin Peninsula, which made the planned landing of the 82nd Airborne Division around St. Saveur-le-Vicomte too risky. Instead, its drop zone was shifted to the Merderet River area, and the 101st Airborne drop zone was shifted slightly south so that both divisions would control an easily defensible area between the beaches and the Douve and Merderet Rivers.

The first troops to land in France in preparation for Operation *Neptune* were OSS teams (Office of Strategic Service), usually consisting of two US soldiers, trained in the operation of signal devices, teamed with three British commandos for site security. A half dozen of these teams were flown into France around 0130hrs on June 3 to mark airborne drop zones for later pathfinder teams who would bring in more extensive marking equipment, including the Eureka beacons. Due to the weather, Operation *Neptune* was delayed a day to June 6, 1944. Before midnight, 19 C-47 aircraft of the

Eisenhower visited with the paratroopers of the 502nd PIR at Greenham Common airbase on the evening of June 5, 1944. The division used playing card symbols on the sides of their helmets to identify the various battalions, the white heart indicating the 502nd PIR. The white cloth band around the left shoulder is believed to be a recognition sign for the 2/502nd PIR. (MHI)

Provisional Pathfinder Group set out for Normandy. On approaching the drop zones, the pathfinder aircraft encountered an unexpected cloudbank that created navigational problems. In the 101st Airborne sector, only the teams allotted to Drop Zone C parachuted close to the target. Likewise in the 82nd Airborne Division sector, only one stick of pathfinders was accurately dropped into Drop Zone O. In the case of the other four drop zones, the pathfinders were dropped so far away from their target that they did not have enough time after their landing to reach their designated drop zone. As a result, some of the pathfinder teams set off their landing beacons in areas away from the planned drop zones, while other teams were able to set up only the Eureka beacons since the presence of German troops nearby made it impossible to set up the Aldis lamps. It was an inauspicious start for the operations.

Operation *Albany*, the delivery of the 101st Airborne Division, was assigned to the 50th and 53rd Troop Carrier Wings, and Operation *Boston*, the delivery of the 82nd Airborne Division, was assigned to the 52nd Wing. The initial wave used 821 C-47 and C-53 transports. The main wave of transports began taking off from England around midnight. In the wake of the Sicily fiasco, the flight path was diverted around the naval task force westward towards the Atlantic then returning eastward, passing between the Channel Islands, and entering enemy airspace over the west Cotentin coast, heading northeastward towards the drop zone, and exiting over Utah Beach. This elongated and complicated flight path was a contributing factor to the navigation problems that plagued the D-Day airdrops.

In parallel to the actual airdrop mission, a force of RAF Stirling bombers flew a diversionary mission, dropping chaff to simulate an airborne formation and dropping dummy paratroopers and noisemakers into areas away from the actual drop zones. The weather conditions were a full moon and clearing skies. The fight proved uneventful until the coast, where the transports encountered the same dense cloudbank that had frustrated the pathfinders. The clouds created immediate dangers due to the proximity of the aircraft in formation, and C-47s began to frantically maneuver to avoid mid-air collisions. Some pilots climbed to 2,000ft to avoid the clouds, others descended below the cloudbank to 500ft, while some remained at the prescribed altitude of 700ft. This cloudbank completely disrupted the formation and ended any hopes for a concentrated paratroop drop. Anti-aircraft fire began during the final approach into the drop zones near the coast. Although they had been instructed to maintain a steady course, some pilots began jinking their aircraft to avoid steady streams of 20mm cannon fire. The airlift was becoming increasingly confused.

Some paratroopers of the 506th PIR, 101st Airborne Division, decided to get Mohican haircuts and daub their faces with their idea of Indian warpaint. This is demolition specialist Clarence Ware applying the finishing touches on Pvt. Charles Plaudo. The censor has obscured the "screaming eagle" divisional patch on his shoulder. (NARA)

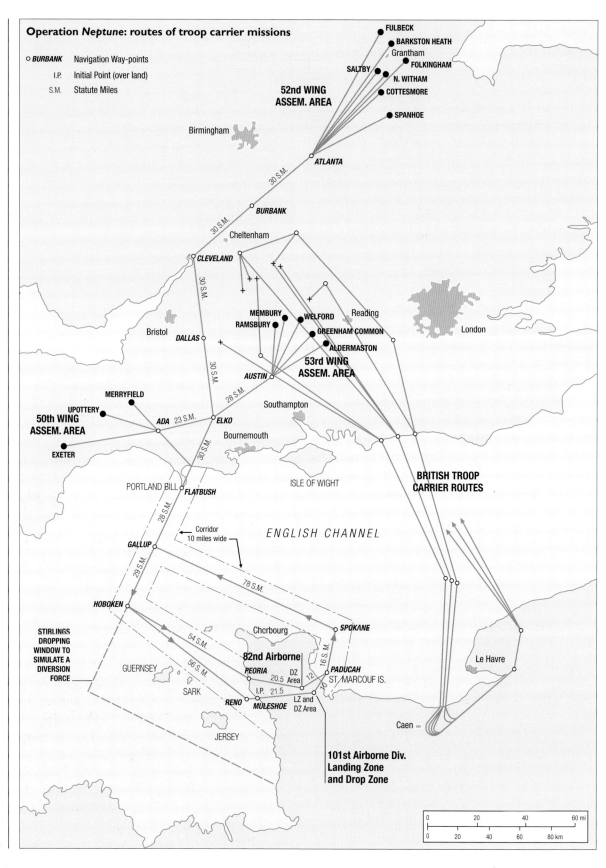

Operation *Neptune*: routes of troop carrier missions

○ *BURBANK*   Navigation Way-points
I.P.   Initial Point (over land)
S.M.   Statute Miles

FULBECK
BARKSTON HEATH
Grantham
FOLKINGHAM
SALTBY
N. WITHAM
COTTESMORE
SPANHOE

52nd WING ASSEM. AREA

Birmingham

30 S.M.

ATLANTA

30 S.M.

BURBANK

Cheltenham

30 S.M.

CLEVELAND

30 S.M.

Reading

MEMBURY
WELFORD
RAMSBURY
GREENHAM COMMON
ALDERMASTON

London

Bristol

DALLAS

53rd WING ASSEM. AREA

30 S.M.

AUSTIN

28 S.M.

Southampton

MERRYFIELD

UPOTTERY

50th WING ASSEM. AREA

ADA   23 S.M.   *ELKO*

EXETER

Bournemouth

30 S.M.

PORTLAND BILL   *FLATBUSH*

ISLE OF WIGHT

BRITISH TROOP CARRIER ROUTES

28 S.M.

Corridor
10 miles wide

ENGLISH CHANNEL

GALLUP

29 S.M.

78 S.M.

HOBOKEN

Cherbourg

SPOKANE

STIRLINGS DROPPING WINDOW TO SIMULATE A DIVERSION FORCE

54 S.M.

16 S.M.

82nd Airborne

PEORIA

DZ Area

PADUCAH

20.5   12

ST. MARCOUF IS.

Le Havre

GUERNSEY

56 S.M.

I.P.   21.5

RENO

MULESHOE

LZ and DZ Area

SARK

Caen

JERSEY

101st Airborne Div. Landing Zone and Drop Zone

0	20	40	60 mi
0	20	40	60	80 km

D-Day airlift operations, IX Troop Carrier Command			
Mission	Albany	Boston	Total
Aircraft sorties	433	378	821
Aborted sorties	2	1	3
Aircraft lost or missing	13	8	21
Aircraft damaged	81	115	196
Aircrew killed or missing	48	17	65
Aircrew wounded	4	11	15
Troops carried	6,928	6,420	13,348
Troops dropped	6,750	6,350	13,100
Howitzers carried	12	2	14
Cargo carried (tons)	211	178	389

Albany mission

The 101st Airborne Division was the first to land around 0130hrs on June 6, 1944. Its primary objective was to seize control of the area behind Utah Beach to facilitate the exit of the 4th Infantry Division from the beach later that morning. Its secondary mission was to protect the southern flank of VII Corps by destroying two bridges on the Carentan Highway and a railroad bridge west of it, gaining control of the Barquette Lock and establishing a bridgehead over the Douve River northeast of Carentan.

The 502nd PIR and 506th PIR (minus one battalion) were assigned to the primary objective. Most of the 2/502nd PIR was dropped compactly, but inaccurately, on the far edge of Drop Zone C, three miles south of the intended Drop Zone A. In spite of the confusion, a detachment moved on the German coastal battery at St. Martin-de-Varreville and, after finding the position deserted, moved on to their next objective, the western side of the Audouville-la-Hubert Causeway (Exit 3), arriving there around 0730hrs and ambushing a German company retreating from the beach. The 1/502nd PIR landed near St. Germain-de-Varreville, with 20 of the 36 aircraft within a mile of the beacon. The 1/502nd PIR held the northern perimeter through D-Day, fighting a number of skirmishes with German troops and sending detachments to link up with the 82nd Airborne near St. Mère Eglise. The 377th Parachute Field Artillery was badly dispersed during landings and only a single howitzer was put into action on D-Day.

A fully loaded paratrooper sometimes needed help to simply move due to the enormous weight of gear and equipment he carried. This is T/4 Joseph Gorenc of the 506th PIR climbing aboard a C-47 on the evening of June 5, 1944. (NARA)

The two battalions of the 506th PIR landed in Drop Zone C. The C-47s passed over a concentration of German flak near Etienville; six aircraft were shot down and 30 damaged. In spite of the fire, some drops were concentrated with one serial of 14 aircraft dropping almost on top of Drop Zone C, and another serial of 13 bunching their sticks a mile and a half east and southeast of the drop zone. But the other serials were much further from their intended targets due to confusion over the beacons. About 140 men of the HQ and 1/506th PIR assembled in the regimental area in the first hours of the landing. The 2/506th PIR landed north of the drop zone and two disconnected groups set out to secure the Houdienville (Exit 2) and Pouppeville (Exit 1) Causeways. Delayed by frequent

Troops of the 325th Glider Infantry prepare to board Horsa gliders at an airfield in England. The US airborne units were provided with the British Horsa gliders to carry larger loads than the Waco CG-4. (NARA)

skirmishes with German troops, the detachments didn't arrive near the beach until the 4th Infantry Division was already moving inland over the causeway.

Next to land was the 3/501st PIR and the divisional HQ, which was to control the planned glider landing area near Hiesville. Gen. Taylor, not in contact with the 506th PIR, sent another detachment to the Pouppeville (Exit 1) Causeway. This was the first of the three paratrooper columns to actually reach the causeway around 0800hrs, but it took nearly four hours for the outnumbered paratroopers to overcome the German defenders in house-to-house fighting. Fighting flared up near the divisional CP in Drop Zone C due to the nearby German Artillery Regiment 191 centered on Ste. Marie-du-Mont. The paratroopers gradually eliminated the batteries, and the town was finally cleared of German troops by mid-afternoon when they were met GIs from the 4th Infantry Division advancing from the beaches.

The final groups to land were the 1/501st PIR, elements of the 2/501st PIR, and the 3/506th PIR as well as engineer and medical personnel. These forces were earmarked for Drop Zone D, the southernmost of the drop zones. The approach to the drop zone was hot, with a considerable amount of light flak, searchlights, and flares. Six C-47s were shot down and 26 damaged. These drops were among the most successful in putting the paratroopers near their intended objective, but this was not entirely a good thing as the Germans had assumed that this area could be used for airborne landings so had troops near the landing zone. In spite of casualties, a detachment from the 1/501st PIR set off for the primary objective, the La Barquette Locks, which controlled the flooding of the areas along the Douve River, and captured them by early morning. The 2/501st PIR was engaged in a sharp firefight with a German infantry battalion and spent most of the day fighting around the town of St. Côme-du-Mont. The third unit landing in Drop Zone D, the 3/506th PIR, had the roughest time. German troops were waiting in the landing area and had soaked a wooden building with fuel. They lit the building on fire, illuminating the descending paratroopers. The battalion commander and his executive officer were among those killed in the first moments. Detachments from the unit managed to fight their way free and seize the bridge at Le Port.

Boston mission

The 82nd Airborne Division's assignment was to land two regiments on the western side of the Mederet River, and one regiment on the eastern side around St. Mère Église to secure the bridges over the Mederet. The landings of the 82nd Airborne were even more badly scattered than those of the 101st Airborne and, as a result, only one of its regiments was able to carry out its assignment on D-Day. The 82nd Airborne began landing about an hour after the 101st Airborne, around 0230hrs.

The 505th PIR was assigned to land on Drop Zone O to the northwest of St. Mère Église. The pathfinders had done such a thorough job marking it that many aircraft circled back over the area to drop the paratroopers more accurately and this proved to be the most accurate series of any of the jumps that night. The 3/505th PIR was assigned to take the town of St. Mère Église and the paratroopers quickly seized it. The 2/505th PIR established a defense line north of the drop zone but when the Germans staged a counterattack against St. Mère Église from the south around 0930hrs most of the battalion was moved to the southern approaches of the town except for a single platoon, which soon became engaged against another attack. The main attack against St. Mère Église was about a battalion in strength, supported by a few StuG III assault guns, but was beaten off. The 1/505th PIR landed with the headquarters including Gen. Ridgway. A group set off for the La Fière Bridge over the Mederet River but an initial attempt to rush the bridge failed due to entrenched German machine-gun teams

The two other regiments of the 82nd Airborne Division landing in Drop Zones T and N on the west side of the Mederet River, were hopelessly scattered. Pathfinders had been unable to mark the drop zones, in some cases due to the proximity of German troops. The transport aircraft were disrupted by the coastal cloudbank, and after arriving over the drop area, the pilots had searched in vain for the signals, or in some cases homed in on the wrong beacon. Much of the 507th PIR was dropped into the marshes east of Drop Zone T while the 508th was dropped south of Drop Zone N. These swamps were deep and many of the heavily laden paratroopers drowned before they could free themselves of their equipment. In addition, a great deal of important equipment and supplies landed in the water, and valuable time had to be spent trying to retrieve this equipment. About half of the 508th PIR landed within two miles of the drop zone, but the remainder landed on the other side of the Mederet River or were scattered to even more distant locations. The 507th PIR dropped in a tighter pattern than the 508th, but many aircraft overshot the drop zone, dumping the paratroopers into the swampy fringes of the Mederet River. The most noticeable terrain feature in the area of the 507th PIR drop was the railroad line from Carentan on an embankment over the marshes. Many paratroopers gathered

An element of the 88th TCS, 438th Troop Carrier Group, passes over the Normandy coast on D-Day with CG-4A gliders in tow during one of the daytime re-supply efforts. (NARA)

along the embankment. A series of confused actions were fought on D-Day attempting to secure the western side of the La Fière Bridge. A group under Gen. Gavin attempted to seize the Chef-du-Pont Bridge but were rebuffed by German troops dug in along the causeway. The fighting for La Fière continued for three days and was the focus of the 82nd Airborne Division's attention.

Glider reinforcements

The next airborne missions in the early hours of D-Day were the glider reinforcement flights: Mission *Detroit* for the 82nd Airborne Division and Mission *Chicago* for the 101st Airborne Division. Mission *Detroit* left England at 0120hrs with 52 Waco C-4A gliders carrying 155 troops, 16 57mm anti-tank guns and 25 jeeps. The nighttime landings at 0345hrs were almost as badly scattered as the paratroopers with only six gliders on target, 15 within a kilometer, ten further west and 18 further east. Nevertheless, casualties were modest with five dead, 17 seriously injured and seven missing, although the 101st Airborne's deputy commander was among those killed in a glider crash. The 46 CG-4A gliders of Mission *Detroit* landed at 0410hrs near the 82nd Airborne's Landing Zone O, carrying 220 troops as well as 22 jeeps and 16 anti-tank guns. About 20 of the gliders landed on or near the landing zone, while seven were released early (five disappearing) and seven more landed on the west bank of the Mederet River. The rough landings in this sector led to the loss of 11 jeeps and most of the gliders, but troop losses were fewer than expected, three dead and 23 seriously injured. The nighttime glider operations were followed by additional reinforcement missions at dusk on D-Day and dawn on D+1 and their results are summarized on the chart below (page 66).

Of the 13,348 paratroops airlifted to Normandy on D-Day, only about 10 percent landed in their intended drop zone, about 25–30 percent within a mile, and 15–20 percent with one to two miles. By H-Hour (0630hrs), the 101st Airborne Division only had 1,100 troops and the 82nd only 1,500 troops near their objectives; by the end of D-Day the 101st only had 2,500 troops and the 82nd only 2,000 troops under divisional control. As a result, neither division was able to fully carry out their intended missions on D-Day, and both divisions were involved in several days of intense fighting after D-Day to secure those objectives. The causes for these problems were varied. Clearly, the navigation technology of the day and the US troop carrier tactics were inadequate. British drops relying on individual navigation and Gee were somewhat better, but neither was a practical option for the US troop carrier force in June 1944. The decision to use a roundabout route to avoid the peril

A jeep of the 506th PIR, 101st Airborne Division, pulls a handcart with supply canister near one of the landing zones off Utah Beach with Horsa gliders evident behind. By this stage, elements of the 4th Infantry Division had arrived as can be seen from the trucks and M29 carrier behind. (NARA)

of naval gunfire was unfortunate as it required more complex navigation, put the serials at greater peril of disruptive cloud cover and exposed the transport serials to more prolonged flak. Beyond the serious dispersion of the drops, the terrain contributed to the problems in assembling the units after landing. The hedgerow terrain along the Normandy coast made assembly difficult and time consuming, and the scattered paratroopers were easily delayed on encountering small German forces.

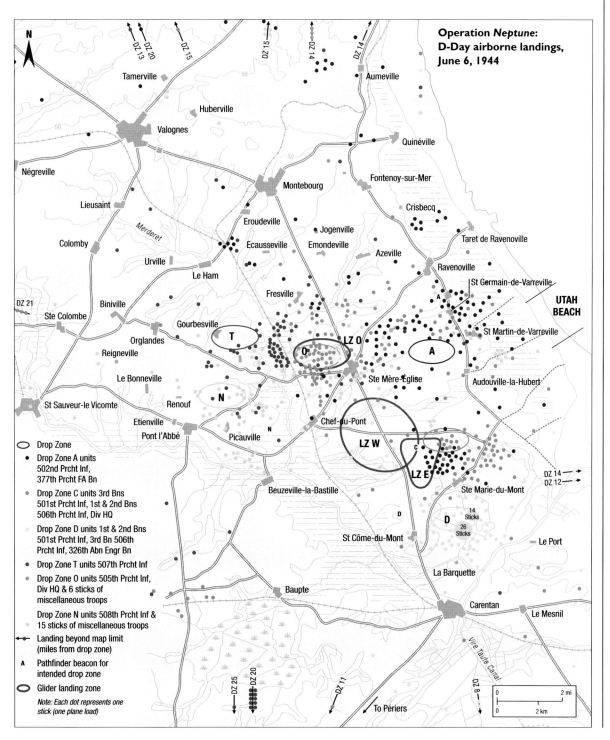

**Operation *Neptune*:
D-Day airborne landings,
June 6, 1944**

Legend:

- ⬭ Drop Zone
- • Drop Zone A units
  502nd Prcht Inf,
  377th Prcht FA Bn
- • Drop Zone C units 3rd Bns
  501st Prcht Inf, 1st & 2nd Bns
  506th Prcht Inf, Div HQ
- Drop Zone D units 1st & 2nd Bns
  501st Prcht Inf, 3rd Bn 506th
  Prcht Inf, 326th Abn Engr Bn
- • Drop Zone T units 507th Prcht Inf
- Drop Zone O units 505th Prcht Inf,
  Div HQ & 6 sticks of
  miscellaneous troops
- Drop Zone N units 508th Prcht Inf &
  15 sticks of miscellaneous troops
- ←• Landing beyond map limit
  (miles from drop zone)
- A Pathfinder beacon for
  intended drop zone
- ⬭ Glider landing zone

*Note: Each dot represents one
stick (one plane load)*

D-Day glider operations, IX Troop Carrier Command							
Mission	Chicago	Detroit	Keokuk	Elmira	Galveston	Hackensack	Total
Mission date	D-Day 0400hrs	D-Day 0407hrs	D-Day 2100hrs	D-Day 2100hrs	D+1 0700hrs	D+1 0900hrs	
Landing zone	LZ E	LZ O	LZ E	LZ W	LZ W	LZ W	
Tow aircraft sorties	52	52	32	177	102	101	516
Aborted sorties	1	0	0	2	2	0	5
Aircraft lost or missing	1	1	0	5	0	0	7
Aircraft damaged	7	38	1	92	26	1	175
Horsa sorties	0	0	32	140	20	30	222
Horsa sorties aborted	0	0	0	2	2	0	4
Waco sorties	52	53	0	36	84	70	295
Waco sorties aborted	1	1	0	0	2	0	4
Aircrew killed or missing	4	4	0	1	0	0	9
Aircrew wounded	1	3	0	8	0	0	12
Glider pilots dispatched	104	106	64	352	208	200	1,034
Glider pilots lost	14	13	0	26	0	3	57
Troops carried	155	220	157	1,190	968	1,331	4,021
Troops landed	153	209	157	1,160	927	1,331	3,937
Waco casualties*	27	30	0	15	35	16	123
Horsa casualties*	0	0	44	142	80	74	340
Artillery carried	16	16	6	37	20	0	95
Vehicles carried	25	27	40	123	41	34	290
Cargo carried (tons)	14	10	19	131	26	38	238

*Troops injured or killed during landing

In spite of problems, the paratroopers managed to accomplish an important portion of their missions largely through their courage, initiative and superior combat efficiency. But at best, the airborne missions were barely successful, and some US commanders, especially Gen. Omar Bradley, were badly disappointed with the results given the amount of effort devoted to these forces.

As was the case with the Sicily mission, the German commanders considered the Allied airborne landings in Normandy to have been a stunning success. The landings led the German 84th Corps to commit their only mobile reserve to tracking down the paratroopers, leaving them without the forces necessary to stage counterattacks against the main Omaha and Utah Beach landings. The Wehrmacht was very confused by the tactics employed, and some German staff officers were convinced that the US airborne was using a cunning new tactic of widespread dispersion to maximize the effect of light forces in undermining defensive positions. Whether they performed their specific missions on time or not, the US airborne divisions completely undermined German defenses behind Utah Beach, and the 4th Infantry Division at Utah suffered lower casualties than on any other D-Day beach. However, airborne casualties had been exceptionally high as the accompanying chart indicates, suffering almost 50 percent casualties from the time of the landing through the subsequent fighting.

The most important lesson of the Normandy airborne operation was the difficulty of night drops given the contemporary state of navigation technology. Even after the formation of the pathfinder units after Sicily, the navigation technology was marginal under the best of circumstances. All subsequent airborne operations in the ETO would be conducted in daylight on the presumption that German flak positions could be suppressed by preliminary air attack and that any remaining air defenses would be no more disruptive or costly to the landing force than the losses and inevitable dispersion caused by night landing. Technical lessons from the operation included the need for self-sealing tanks on the C-47 transport aircraft, and the need for a quick-release harness for the combat parachute. As mentioned in the organization section above, the Normandy operation reinforced the tendency to shift to a two parachute/one glider configuration as well as the need to enhance the support elements of the division.

US airborne casualties D-Day to July 1, 1944					
Unit	Killed	Wounded	Missing	Captured	Total
82nd Abn. Div.	457	1,440	2,571	12+	4,480
101st Abn. Div	546	2,217	1,907	?	4,670
Total	1,003	3,657	4,478	12	9,150

Operation *Dragoon*: the champagne campaign

The next airborne operation in the ETO was in support of the Operation *Dragoon* amphibious landings on the French Riviera coast on 15 August. This operation is covered in detail in Gordon Rottman's *Battle Orders 22: US Airborne in the Mediterranean Theater 1942–45* (Osprey: Oxford, 2006), so the discussion here will be brief. The mission of Rugby Force was to serve as a buffer between the amphibious landings and any German mobile reserve, especially along the main highway heading towards St. Raphael and the shoreline. The principal airborne component of this operation was an improvised airborne division variously called the Seventh Army Provisional Airborne Division, or the 1st Provisional Airborne Task Force. This consisted of the British 2nd Independent Parachute Brigade, the 517th PIR, the 509th and 551st Parachute Infantry Battalions, and the 550th Glider Infantry Battalion. The unit was commanded by Maj. Gen. Robert Frederick, who had previously commanded the joint Canadian–American 1st Special Service Force in the Italian campaign. The air element of Rugby Force was the Provisional Troop Carrier Division, headed on a temporary basis by Brig. Gen. Paul Williams, commander of IX Troop Carrier Command during the Normandy operation. About a third of IX Troop Carrier Command was diverted to Italy for the operation and included 512 C-47s from the 50th, 51st and 53rd Troop Carrier Wings.

Glider infantry of the 1st Airborne Task Force exit their CG-4A assault glider near La Motte on the French Riviera coast on August 15, 1944, during Operation *Dragoon*. (NARA)

A deception operation northwest of Toulon preceded the Rugby Force airdrop. Three pathfinder teams jumped over the Le Muy area around 0330hrs on August 15 with plans to set up Eureka beacons supplemented by radio compass homing beacons. Ground fog over the target area led to a badly scattered pathfinder jump, with only one of the three teams landing in its assigned drop zone. In spite of this problem, the 396 transport aircraft had an uneventful night flight into the target area around Le Muy as the Navy had provided shipboard additional navigation beacons along the way that helped improve the accuracy of the landings. The parachute jumps began around dawn at 0430hrs and about 60 percent of the paratroopers landed in their intended drop zones or nearby, a substantial improvement over the Normandy experience. The initial glider landings, codenamed Operation *Bluebird*, were supposed to begin around 0800hrs with an initial force of 40 CG-4A and 35 Horsa gliders. *Bluebird* was delayed until 0900hrs by thick ground fog and the Horsa wave was sent back to base. The CG-4A glider landings were successfully executed and brought in jeeps, artillery and supplies. The Rugby Force proceeded to fan out and seize nearby towns and villages. The airborne force was reinforced in the afternoon by Operation *Dove*, a further 332 CG-4A gliders plus the returning Horsas carrying about 2,500 troops and more heavy equipment. The landings started around 1830hrs and at one point there were some 180 gliders in free flight over the landing zones. The fighting with the neighboring German garrisons was light, and by the afternoon of D+1, August 16, the paratroopers and glider infantry made contact with the 45th Division, which had landed on Red Beach in the center of the coast the morning before. Elements of the 509th Parachute Battalion were erroneously dropped near St. Tropez but captured the resort town prior to the arrival of the 3rd Infantry Division. In total, the air operation had conducted 987 sorties including 407 CG-4A gliders and had delivered 9,000 troops, 221 jeeps and 213 artillery and other heavy weapons. The 1st Provisional Airborne Task Force was subsequently assigned to cover the right flank of the Seventh Army advance, liberating the cities of Cannes and Nice. Overall, the Operation *Dragoon* airborne landing had gone remarkably smoothly, in no small measure due to the weak German response and the growing experience of the troop carriers and airborne units.

Operation *Market*: paving the way to a bridge too far

With the organization of the First Allied Airborne Army underway, SHAEF and the airborne staffs began considering follow-on airborne operations to employ the growing Allied airborne force. Most of those planned in July were short-lived schemes to assist in the Normandy breakout but they were made moot by

Troops of the 82nd Division headquarters company prepare to load aboard a C-47 of the 44th TCS, 316th TCW at Cottesmore on September 17, 1944, at the start of Operation *Market*. (NARA)

the rapidity of the US Army's advance after Operation *Cobra* began on July 24. Once the German Army in the west began collapsing in mid-August, the next set of schemes involved efforts to conduct a deep envelopment of retreating forces by dropping airborne forces in their path of retreat in Belgium. Once again, the pace of the ground campaign outpaced the planning and these schemes were quickly forgotten. The plans became more serious towards the end of August and British and Polish airborne units were actually deployed to airfields for some of these operations including *Linnet* and a portion of the troop carrier force sequestered to provide the necessary airlift.

Linnet was canceled on September 5, to be followed by a more ambitious scheme codenamed *Comet*, which envisioned a complex operation to seize a Rhine River bridge at Arnhem in the Netherlands on the German border northwest of the Ruhr industrial region. The British 1st Airborne Division and Polish Parachute Brigade would seize bridges over the Maas at Grave, over the Waal at Nijmegen and over the Rhine at Arnhem. US airborne engineers were

Canceled First Airborne Army operations, summer 1944

Codename	Planned date	Drop zone	Airborne unit	Mission
Wildoats	June 14	Evrecy	British 1st Airborne Division	Clear the way for British 7th Armoured Division attack
Hands Up	mid-July	Quiberon Bay	Undetermined	Seize ports
Beneficiary	mid-July	St. Malo	Undetermined	Seize port
Swordhilt	end of July	Brest	Undetermined	Seize port
Transfigure	August 17	Orléans gap	US 101st, UK 1st Abn. Div., Polish Bde.	Trap German Seventh Army
Boxer	end of August	Boulogne	Undetermined	Seize port, harass retreating German forces
Linnet	September 2–3	Tournai	US 82nd, 101st, UK 1st Abn. Div.; Polish Bde.	Cut off retreating Germans
Linnet II	September 4–6	Liège	US 82nd, 101st, UK 1st Abn. Div.; Polish Bde.	Seize Meuse River crossing
Comet	September 8	Arnhem	Undetermined	Seize Rhine bridges from Arnhem to Wesel
Infatuate	September	Walcheren Island	Undetermined	Assist Canadian Army to clear access to Antwerp
Naples I	September	East of Aachen	XVIII Airborne Corps	Assist First Army break through the Siegfried Line
Naples II	September	Cologne area	XVIII Airborne Corps	Seize Rhine bridge in Cologne area
Milan I	September	Trier area	XVIII Airborne Corps	Assist Third Army to penetrate Siegfried line
Milan II	September	Koblenz area	XVIII Airborne Corps	Assist in Rhine crossing in Neuweid-Koblenz area
Choker I	September	Saarbrucken	XVIII Airborne Corps	Assist Seventh Army to break through Siegfried Line
Choker II	September	Mannheim	XVIII Airborne Corps	Assist a crossing of the Rhine between Mainz and Mannheim
Talisman	September	Berlin	Undetermined	In the event of a sudden German collapse, seize Berlin airfields and naval base at Kiel

The US airborne landings were intended to pave the way for the armored columns of the British XXX Corps. Here, two paratroopers of the 82nd Airborne Division talk to the crew of a British Stuart light tank of the Sherwood Rangers Yeomanry, 8th Armoured Brigade, which provided armored support in late September and early October. (MHI)

to prepare a forward airfield and the British 52nd Lowland Division (Airportable) would then be landed to reinforce the airborne advance. Although *Comet* was canceled on September 10, Eisenhower had already come out in favor of using the First Allied Airborne Army to assist Montgomery's 21st Army Group in a rapid race to the Rhine, giving it priority over other options such as Patton's advance through Lorraine towards Frankfurt. *Comet* was modified to incorporate the US XVIII Airborne Corps, with the airborne mission codenamed Operation *Market*, and the ground assault by the British XXX Corps, supported by VIII and XII Corps, designated *Garden*. The new assignments were to land the 101st Airborne Division near Eindhoven to clear a path for the advance of the armored divisions of the British XXX Corps; land the 82nd Airborne Division around Nijmegen to seize the Waal River bridges there; and land the British 1st Airborne Division near Arnhem to seize a Rhine bridge, with plans to drop the Polish Parachute Brigade as reinforcements once airlift became available. The plans expected the XXX Corps to reach the Arnhem Bridge by D+3 or +4. In view of the problems experienced in Normandy with night landings, Operation *Market* was scheduled to take place on the afternoon of September 17, with an elaborate tactical air plan to suppress German flak positions.

The US airborne commanders were disturbed by the initial British plans which they felt were too hastily conceived. Gen. Taylor was deeply uneasy with the idea that the 101st Airborne would capture and control a pathway some 30 miles long from the forward Allied lines through Eindhoven and beyond towards Nijmegen.

Glider infantry of the 327th GIR, 101st Airborne Division, move off Landing Zone W near Son on September 18, 1944, (D+1) while a jeep from the regimental service company passes by. (NARA)

In the event, Taylor spoke to the commander of the British XXX Corps, Lt. Gen. Miles Dempsey, about this and he agreed that there was no urgent need for the paratroopers from Eindhoven south, which made the objectives difficult but possible. Gen. Gavin was less concerned with the overall plan than in the particulars, and one significant change was to place the landing of the 504th PIR closer to the Maas River bridge near Grave, including a company immediately on the bridge's western approach. In contrast to the Normandy mission, Operation *Market*'s tactical planning was more than a little slapdash and impromptu, with very little training of the airborne units possible. British assessments of likely German reactions were too optimistic and US commanders were very surprised to learn that the British 1st Airborne Division planned to land eight miles from the Arnhem Bridge instead of nearby this key objective.

The airlift operation was complicated by the need to fly from bases in England since bases in France were being used by tactical aviation. This was somewhat ameliorated by Brereton's arrangement to borrow 250 B-24 bombers to conduct a major re-supply effort on D+2, but it weakened the strength of the initial landings during the first few days of good weather. This complex battle has been described in detail many times, and the focus here will be the US XVIII Airborne Corps efforts in the Eindhoven–Nijmegen area.

The initial 101st Airborne Division force was carried to the Netherlands in 428 transports and 70 gliders on the afternoon of September 17, 1944. The main landing area was located north of Eindhoven and west of Son, consisting of Drop Zone B for the 502nd PIR, Drop Zone C for the 506th PIR and Landing Zone W for the gliders. The 501st PIR landed further north in two separate drop zones, A and A-1 to the southwest and northwest of Veghel on the Aa River. The 501st PIR landing was not entirely accurate, but the main objectives of the four bridges over the Aa River and the Willemsvaart Canal were quickly seized. The 502nd PIR seized the bridge over the Dommel River at St. Oedenrode and over the Wilhelmina Canal near Best, but the Best Canal bridge was recaptured by a German counterattack before dark. The 506th PIR moved on Son where two of the bridges had already been blown the week before, and the Germans detonated the remaining bridge before the paratroopers could capture it. Nevertheless, the 506th PIR was able to establish control of the town on both sides of the Wilhelmina Canal by nightfall, waiting for the next day to link up with XXX Corps near Eindhoven.

The 82nd Airborne Division was carried into action by 400 transport aircraft and 50 gliders including 7,277 paratroopers and 209 glider infantry. The 504th PIR landed in two drop zones on either side of Grave and its Maas River bridge, taking the Grave Bridge (Bridge 11) before dusk. The regiment was also tasked with capturing the western side of four other bridges along the Maas–Waal Canal in conjunction with other units of the division from the eastern side. The southernmost bridge (Bridge 7) was captured, the ones north of Malden (Bridge 8) and Hatert (Bridge 9) were blown by the Germans, and the damaged bridge at Honinghutie was seized the following day (Bridge 10). The 505th PIR

A dramatic view from Landing Zone W around 1430hrs on D+1 (September 18, 1944), as CG-4A assault gliders land near Son. (NARA)

71

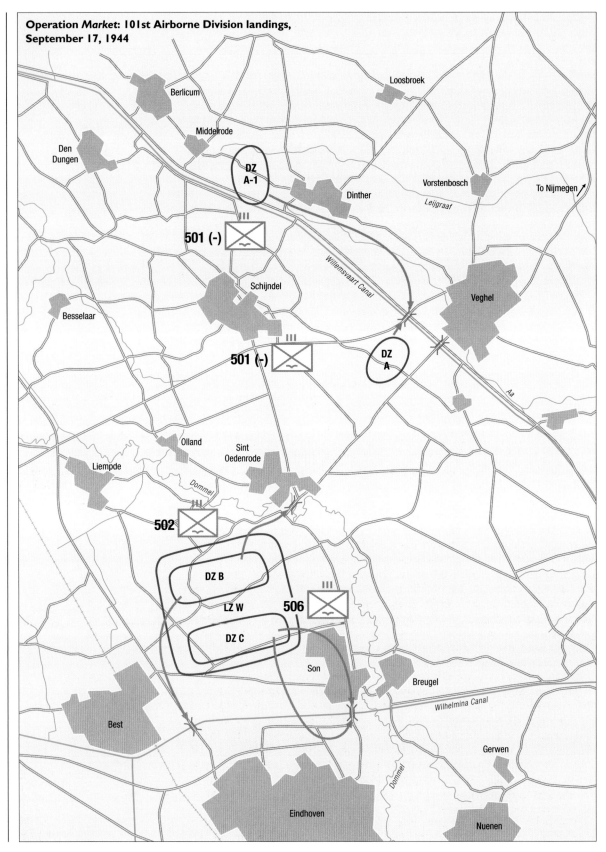

Operation *Market*: 101st Airborne Division landings,
September 17, 1944

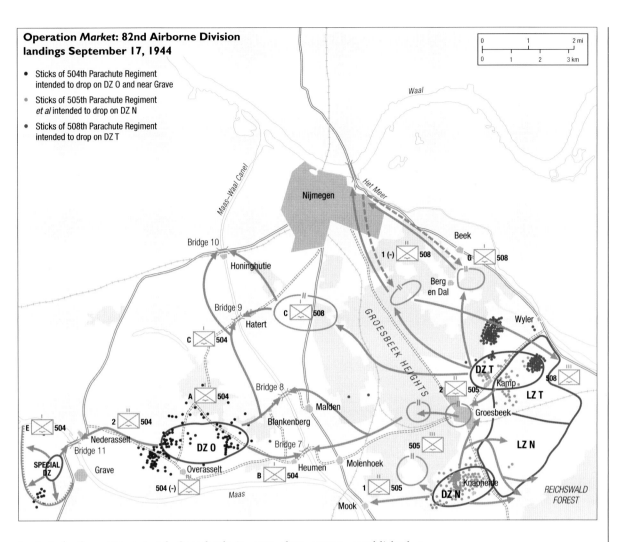

Operation *Market*: 82nd Airborne Division landings September 17, 1944

- Sticks of 504th Parachute Regiment intended to drop on DZ O and near Grave
- Sticks of 505th Parachute Regiment *et al* intended to drop on DZ N
- Sticks of 508th Parachute Regiment intended to drop on DZ T

landed further east around Groesbeek in two drop zones, established a defensive perimeter towards the Reichswald to the southeast and linked up with the 504th PIR along the Maas–Waal Canal. The Germans had already demolished the railroad bridge on the northwest side of Mook. The 508th PIR landed northeast of Groesbeek and its principal mission was to seize and control the high ground west of Berg en Dal including Hill 95.6, which dominated the flat Dutch landscape in the area. This was accomplished and two companies reached to within 400 yards of the Nijmegen road bridge. This bridge was not an immediate objective of the first day's plans and the companies stopped after meeting fierce resistance.

Overall, the first day's operation had been a considerable success compared to the Normandy drops. Fighter-bombers had managed to suppress German flak positions and losses totaled 35 transport aircraft and 13 gliders, less than six percent of the troop carrier contingent. The pathfinders had generally been successful, and while not all the landings were on the drop zones, they were close enough that the divisions did not have undue trouble assembling their forces. The Wehrmacht did not anticipate the airborne attack so resistance on the first day was light. The fighting would intensify dramatically over the next few days as the Germans attempted to stamp out the landings, attacking the Allied forces on all sides of the salient.

The 101st Airborne Division pressed south towards Eindhoven on the morning of September 18, while the British Guards Armoured Division pressed north. The paratroopers captured the city by early afternoon and linked up with the British tanks in the evening around 1900hrs. After quickly bridging the Wilhelmina Canal in the dark, the Guards Armored Division crossed around dawn on September 19 and raced up to the 82nd Airborne Division sector by 0820hrs. Combined British and American attacks to seize the vital Nijmegen Bridge were repulsed through September 19 due to the arrival of elements of the 10th SS-Panzer Division from the Arnhem area. But in a bold move, the 82nd Airborne outflanked the defenses on the afternoon of September 20 by using boats to cross a mile downstream from the bridge. Last-minute German attempts to detonate the bridge failed and British tanks were streaming over the bridge that night, heading for Arnhem.

Nevertheless, the delays caused by the initial defense at Eindhoven, the need to build a bridge at Son, and the fighting for the bridge at Nijmegen had slowed the advance by XXX Corps and put it behind schedule. German resistance against the 1st Airborne Division in Arnhem was far fiercer than anticipated due to the unexpected presence of two Waffen-SS panzer divisions refitting in the area. The poor weather after the first day, combined with radio problems, made it difficult and sometimes impossible to conduct supply drops to the encircled British paratroopers, and most of the supplies ended up falling into German-controlled areas. By the time that XXX Corps reached the approaches to Arnhem on September 21, the situation in the city was dire. The surviving airborne troops holding the western side of the bridge were forced to retreat that day to the main concentration of the 1st Airborne Division but were unable to do so and were killed or fell prisoner. With resistance intensifying all around the Allied salient by September 22, the British Second Army gave permission to withdraw forces if necessary. The positions of the 1st Airborne Division were untenable and permission to withdraw was given on September 25, with the action taking place on the night of September 25–26. The Allied positions in the Netherlands were so tenuous, and the German counterattacks so vigorous, that initial plans to withdraw the two US airborne divisions at the conclusion of Operation *Market* were continually frustrated. Both divisions were reinforced by landing administrative units and additional vehicles in Normandy by sea and then sending them by road into the combat zone. In addition, both divisions had an assortment of British units attached to them. The Canadian II Corps did not arrive in the Netherlands until November, and so the 82nd Airborne Division remained in the line until November 11–13, and the 101st Airborne Division until November 25–27.

US airborne casualties, Operation *Market*: September 17–October 16, 1944				
Unit	Killed	Wounded	Missing	Total
82nd Airborne Division	336	1,912	661	2,909
101st Airborne Division	573	1,987	378	2,938
Total	909	3,899	1,039	5,847

The failure of Operation *Market-Garden* can be traced to numerous factors, in many cases too complex to examine in this short survey. The operation was inherently risky, presuming that the crisis in the Wehrmacht would last through September and beyond. The basic strategic premise was proven to be incorrect and, instead of collapsing, the German forces in Holland resisted much more fiercely than expected. The violent German reaction in Arnhem was unanticipated due to the failure to recognize that the 2nd SS-Panzer Corps was refitting in the area. Besides these fundamental planning misjudgments, the airborne operation had important lessons. The decision to use a daylight drop proved fully justified as it contributed significantly to the accuracy of the

Troops of the 506th PIR scramble to free the crew trapped in a CG-4A glider of the 84th TCS on Landing Zone W, which was involved in a mid-air collision with another glider after one of the pilots was wounded in the face by flak. (NARA)

drops and the speed in assembling the forces on the ground. The most serious shortcoming of the troop carrier operation was the time it took to deliver the forces. Due to the range from England, the lack of forward airfields in France and the shortage of aircrews, the transports could only fly one sortie per day. The delivery of the three divisions was extended over a period of three days as a result, which seriously compromised the operation. For example, the need to guard the landing areas and drop zones for later waves of troops forced the ground commanders to divert as much as a third of their forces to this secondary task, weakening their attacks. Poor weather further contributed to the stretch-out of the later drops intended for D+2 and the Polish 1st Airborne Brigade was not delivered until D+4, while the 325th GIR was not delivered until D+6. Had the Poles been present at Arnhem sooner, it might have affected the fighting for the bridge. Had the 325th GIR been present near Nijmegen sooner, it might have permitted a more rapid seizure of the bridge, facilitating the advance of the British XXX Corps armored columns. Yet even if the bridge at Arnhem been seized and held, it is by no means clear that the strategic objective of the mission would have been attained since the Rhine crossing was

The B-24 Liberator bomber was used on several occasions to supplement transport aircraft for dropping supplies during airborne operations as is seen here in September 1944 during Operation *Market*. This required the bottom ball-turret to be removed to create a suitable opening for the para-pack drop. (Patton Museum)

merely the means to inject Montgomery's 21st Army Group into the Ruhr industrial area to outflank the Siegfried Line. With the Wehrmacht rapidly recovering from the summer disaster and the Allies' logistical links overstretched, a deep penetration into Germany before the onset of winter was doubtful, whether the Arnhem Bridge was captured or not.

From the airborne perspective, Brereton already understood the need for forward airfields to facilitate airborne operations on the Continent and attempted to establish a troop carrier center around Reims prior to Operation *Market*. This could not be accomplished until the autumn due to the commitment of so much of the troop carrier force to Operation *Dragoon* and *Market* in quick succession, as well as the continual diversion of the force for forward airlift of fuel and supplies. In addition to forward basing, Brereton also accelerated training in glider double-tow, which would enable the limited transport force to substantially increase the number of gliders delivered. Although this had been demonstrated in 1943, the poor performance of this tactic in Burma in early 1944 had discouraged its use in Europe through most of 1944.

IX Troop Carrier Command missions for Operation *Market* September 17–23, 1944*						
Date	Sep 17	Sep 18	Sep 19	Sep 20	Sep 21	Sep 23
Aircraft (parachute)	910	126	60	357	63	0
Aircraft (gliders)	120	904	385	0	0	490
Aircraft lost	34	20	19	0	0	9
Aircraft damaged	279	241	185	11	0	96
Gliders dispatched	120	904	385	0	0	490
Gliders landed	110	853	225	0	0	430
Paratroops carried	14,009	2,119	0	125	0	0
Paratroops landed	13,941	2,110	0	125	0	0
Glider infantry carried	527	4,397	2,310	0	0	3,773
Glider Infantry landed	506	4,255	1,363	0	0	3,350
Troops landed total	14,447	6,365	1,363	125	0	3,350
Cargo carried (tons, para+glider)	414+87	51+455	71+245	489	16	348

*Does not include US missions for British and Polish airborne units

A recurring controversy raised again by Operation *Market* was the use of US glider pilots after landing. The British practice was to form them into their own company and use them as reinforcing infantry if necessary. The US practice of evacuating them as soon as possible proved unworkable and the presence of so many unarmed personnel was at times more of a hindrance than a help. In practice, the glider pilots often volunteered as infantry, but there was no organized system and the pilots received inadequate infantry training. This led to a decision to provide some training and organization for future operations.

Allied airborne operations in the wake of Operation *Market-Garden* were inhibited by Montgomery's insistence that the two US divisions remain in the line for an extended period to assist the British Second Army in the Netherlands until other infantry became available. Since both the British 1st and 6th Airborne Divisions were refitting after suffering heavy losses in Normandy and at Arnhem, and the US 13th and 17th Airborne Divisions were still stateside, there were no airborne forces to conduct airborne missions. By late autumn, the Allied armies were conducting very limited offensive operations after having outrun their logistical capabilities. Bradley wanted to revive Operation *Choker II*, an operation between Mainz and Mannheim to support the US Seventh Army, but the resources were not available.

During the crisis in the Ardennes in December 1944, the two airborne divisions were the US Army's only available reserve. Here, the 2/504th PIR advances near Cheneux, Belgium, on December 22, 1944. To the right is an airborne 6-pdr, a lightweight British counterpart to the 57mm anti-tank gun used by the airborne divisions. (NARA)

Attention briefly shifted to potential operations in the late winter when major offensives over the Rhine were anticipated. In the event, the unanticipated German offensive in the Ardennes starting on December 17, 1944, forced the commitment of the 82nd, 101st and newly arrived 17th Airborne Divisions since they were the only reserve available to Bradley's 12th Army Group. Although they had not completed their refitting, the 82nd and 101st were rapidly shipped by truck from Reims to Belgium, in many cases without adequate winter clothing or sufficient ammunition. The 101st Airborne Division was assigned to defend the little-known town of Bastogne at a key road junction on the approaches to the Meuse River, one of the key German objectives.[2] The defense of Bastogne became the 101st Airborne Division's most legendary combat action. One of the few airborne elements to the battle was the use of the troop carriers to lift supplies to the besieged town, including a number of small glider lifts to bring in supplies and medics. The 82nd Airborne Division, along with XVIII Airborne Corps headquarters, was assigned the St. Vith sector further to the northeast. By the time it had arrived, the advance of the Sixth Panzer Army had already been stymied but there was still hard fighting ahead through the remainder of December and early January 1945. The 17th Airborne Division saw its combat debut in the Ardennes, being sent into the line in January 1945 during the efforts to reduce the bulge. The desperate shortage of infantry forced the commitment of other paratroop units including a number of separate battalions and regiments. The 517th PIR, later part of the 13th Airborne Division, was deployed to support the 3rd Armored Division in the fighting in the St. Vith sector in December 1944.

Operation *Varsity*: bouncing the Rhine

The final airborne operation in the ETO was conducted in March 1945 as part of the Allied offensive over the Rhine River. Several potential airborne operations were considered as part of this campaign of which Operation *Varsity* was the only one actually conducted. SHAEF tasked the First Allied Airborne Army to plan Operation *Jubilant*, a potential mission to protect prisoner-of-war camps due to the fear of Nazi atrocities in the final days of the war. The most ambitious proposal in 1945 was Operation *Arena*, a scheme unveiled on March 12 to deploy XVIII Airborne Corps into the Kassel area behind the German Rhine defenses, establish a defensive zone, then fly in additional infantry divisions for a grand total of ten divisions to create a "New Front" to wage operations into the heart of Germany. Although Eisenhower expressed

---

2 For further details, the combat actions of the 82nd Airborne Division are described in *Campaign 115: Battle of the Ardennes 1944 (1): St. Vith and the Northern Shoulder* (Osprey: Oxford, 2003) and the 101st Airborne Division in *Campaign 145, Battle of the Bulge (2): Bastogne* (Osprey: Oxford, 2004).

Landing Zone South is crowded with CG-4A gliders and troops of the 194th Glider Infantry Regiment on March 24, 1945 during the Operation *Varsity* landings north of Wesel. (MHI)

enthusiasm, the First US Army breakout from the Remagen bridgehead on March 24, 1945, was so rapid that that an airborne operation proved unnecessary. Patton's Third Army also considered an improvised airborne operation, airlifting infantry over the Rhine in the Frankfurt area using available light liaison aircraft. This also proved unnecessary due to the rapid advance in this sector by more conventional means. Indeed, the airborne element of Operation *Varsity* took place in spite of crumbling German defenses along the Rhine more due to inertia than necessity. Operation *Talisman* was dusted off in this period, renamed *Eclipse*. It was intended to land an airborne force near Berlin in the event of a German collapse, or an airborne assault if the Germans moved the government from Berlin during the Russian siege to some other city such as Munich.

The first staff study for an airborne landing over the Rhine was completed as early as November 7, 1944. The Battle of the Bulge intervened, and Montgomery's 21st Army Group did not fight its way out of the Reichswald until February 1945, putting it along the Rhine by early March 1945. The initial version of Operation *Varsity* assumed an airborne landing in advance of Operation *Plunder*, the main river crossing. This plan included three divisions, the British 6th and US 13th and 17th Airborne Divisions. The first change came when the commander of the British Second Army recommended staging it shortly after *Plunder*, with an aim to speed the penetration of the German defenses north of the Ruhr around Wesel. Brereton did not want a repeat of the staggered landings of Operation *Market*, but instead preferred a fast, hard punch, with the main airdrops lasting only four hours instead of several days. Since the troop carrier force had a limited capacity, this meant landing only two divisions, the British 6th and the US 17th Airborne Divisions, instead of the planned three.

Under the revised *Varsity* plan, IX Troop Carrier Command provided all the airlift of the 17th Airborne Division as well as the paratroopers of the British 6th Airborne Division, while British squadrons towed the British gliders. To further speed the drop, the mission included a few technical innovations including the first use of double-tow gliders in Northwest Europe, the introduction of the larger C-46 Commando transport in this theater for airborne operations, and the first glider landings conducted without preliminary paratrooper drops on the glider landing zones to secure them. The proximity of First Allied Airborne Army fields in nearby France and Belgium allowed the largest single airborne assault to date with 699 transports and 429 gliders carrying the British 6th Airborne Division from England and 903 transports and 897 gliders carrying the US 17th Airborne Division from France and Belgium. The mission also included a massive aerial support operation including fighter sweeps by 1,253 fighters of the US Eighth Air Force and 900 of the RAF Second Tactical Air Force, with a further 213 RAF fighters escorting the transports from England and 676 fighters escorting the US airlift from France.

Operation *Varsity* began at 0600hrs on March 24 but, in spite of ample pre-invasion bombardment, the heavy German flak concentrations in the area accounted for 54 US transports and gliders shot down and 440 damaged. The greatest problem was not the heavy flak since the formations dropped the paratroopers at 600ft, but rather the 20mm flak, which accounted for three-quarters of the aircraft damage and losses. The landing areas were tightly bunched and included four paratroop drop zones and six glider landings zones. German troops in the area were mainly from the 84th Infantry Division, which, curiously enough, had fought the 82nd Airborne Division around Nijmegen several months before. By March 1945, it had been badly beaten up by the British XXX Corps in the February fighting in the Reichswald. The drop zones were in the 84th Infantry Division's rear and contained numerous divisional flak and artillery units as well as support troops. It was being supported by Sturmgeschütz Brigade 394, which had 22 StuG III assault guns and four tanks on hand at the time.

The pathfinder aircraft were led by Col. Joel Crouch, who had helped establish the original pathfinder group, and accompanied by Col. Edson Raff, commander of the 507th PIR, who had led the first paratroop missions in North Africa as well as participating in many of the airborne operations in 1944. The initial jump started at 0953hrs with 1/507th PIR landing about 2,000 yards northwest of the intended Drop Zone W. This was due to poor visibility on the ground caused by smoke pots along the Rhine being used to shield the British amphibious assault mingling with a pall of smoke from nearby Wesel, which had been heavily bombed. This had little consequence, as the battalion's mission was to secure the western edge of the Diersfordter Woods, which

There was some intermingling of British and US gliders in the congested landing zones of Operation *Varsity*. In the foreground is an American CG-4A nicknamed "Cornfield Clipper," while beyond it is a British Horsa and another American CG-4A is to the left. (MHI)

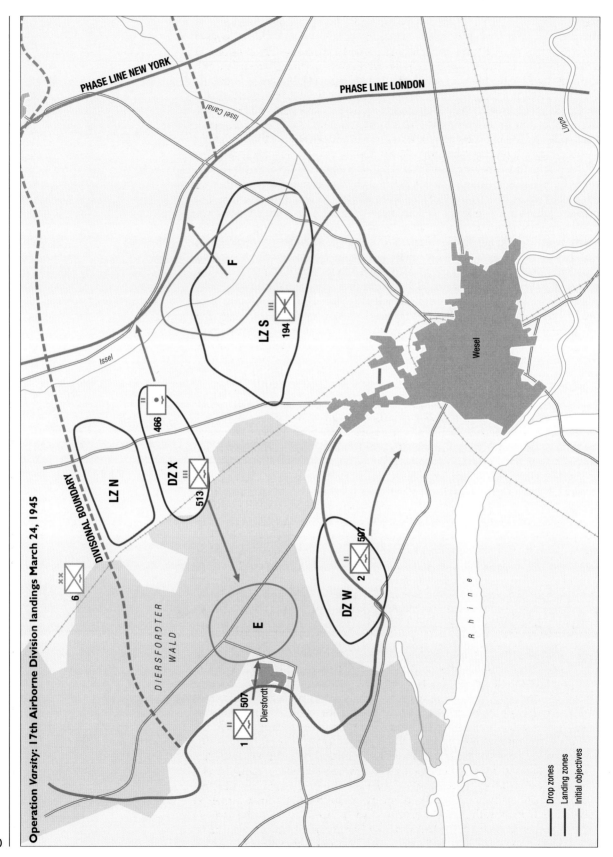

Operation *Varsity*: 17th Airborne Division landings March 24, 1945

PHASE LINE NEW YORK

PHASE LINE LONDON

Issel Canal

Lippe

Issel

F

LZ S

194

466

DZ X

513

LZ N

DIVISONAL BOUNDARY

6

DIERSFORDTER WALD

E

DZ W

507

2

Rhine

507

1

Diersfordt

Wesel

— Drop zones
— Landing zones
— Initial objectives

they promptly occupied, capturing a German 150mm artillery battery and numerous prisoners in the process. The following 2/507th and 3/507th landed in DZ W and proceeded to storm Diersfordt Castle, knocking out five German assault guns in the process including two with the new 75mm recoilless rifles. The 464th Parachute Field Artillery Battalion arrived in DZ W around 1000hrs and began shelling German positions in the nearby woods. The regiment had 90 percent of its troops assembled within an hour and half from the first jump. In less than four hours, the 507th PIR accomplished all of its missions against a numerically superior force and in the process captured over 1,000 prisoners.

The serials delivering the 513th PIR encountered poor visibility conditions after crossing the Rhine, and the lead C-46 transport of the 313th Troop Carrier Group was set on fire by flak but continued to lead the formation. This formation was particularly hard hit by flak, and the C-46 displayed an alarming propensity to catch fire even after minor hits. The 513th PIR landed about 2,000 yards northeast of DZ X in the area intended for the British 6th Airborne Division. This regiment landed against stiffer resistance than the 507th PIR and spent the rest of the morning clearing resistance as they moved south to their intended objectives. In the process, the regiment captured 1,152 German troops and knocked out three StuG III assault guns and two 88mm guns. The regiment reached the intended drop zone by early afternoon. The supporting 466th Parachute Field Artillery Battalion had the misfortune of landing accurately on DZ X only to find it a hive of German activity. The battalion assembled their howitzers under intense fire and began engaging targets of opportunity. They were assisted by a single stick of paratroopers who had landed in the proper drop zone, as well as glider infantry who had landed in the nearby LZ N. During the course of the fighting, the battalion killed 50 German troops and captured 320, along with 18 machine guns, eight 20mm Flak and ten 76mm artillery pieces. The battalion was in touch by radio with the 513th PIR and was in the curious position of providing fire support towards the paratroopers as they moved southward against German troops, located between the pack howitzer batteries and the regiment.

The 53rd Wing followed with the gliders, beginning the releases over LZ-S around 1030hrs. Flak and small-arms fire was intense and of the 295 aircraft on the way to LZ S, 12 were shot down and 140 damaged. Flak and small-arms fire seemed to be heaviest against the gliders, and only about a third of the gliders escaped being hit but fewer than a half-dozen actually crashed. In spite of the intense ground fire, the landings were accurate, except for one group that landed northwest of LZ S, which fortunately was occupied by other US troops. LZ S was hot, with numerous German infantry, several 20mm Flak batteries, four artillery pieces and numerous mortars. Nine gliders were destroyed on the ground by gunfire and several others were hit on landing by machine-gun fire, wounding most of the glider infantry on board. The 194th GIR fought an intense but disjointed battle to control the landing zone for nearly two hours, finally managing to assemble about three-quarters of its troops by noon. A counterattack was attempted against the southern edge of the landing zone, spearheaded by tanks and StuG III assault guns. The Panzers overran some of the positions of Company G, but four were knocked out with bazookas and the attacks petered out by evening. A patrol was sent southward around dusk to make contact with the British 1st Commando Brigade advancing near Wesel. The Germans staged another attack from the Wesel area around midnight, running into a defensive position manned by an improvised company of glider pilots of the 435th Group reinforced by two batteries from the anti-aircraft battalion. The Germans stumbled into the defenses in the dark and were hit by point-blank fire, with one assault gun and 50 troops being lost in an intense skirmish. While retreating, the German force bumped into another glider infantry position, suffering further losses and bringing the attacks to a halt. During the course of the day's fighting, the 194th GIR in LZ S took 1,150 prisoners and destroyed or captured ten armored vehicles, two self-propelled flak guns, 37 artillery pieces and ten 20mm Flak guns at a cost of about 50 dead and 100 wounded infantry, and about 20 dead and 80 wounded glider pilots.

The final landing of the attack was by gliders on LZ N, mainly carrying the division's support troops. The approach to this landing zone was relatively quiet compared to earlier landings as the earlier landings had already overcome most of the heaviest German flak concentrations. However, small-arms fire from LZ N was intense as paratroopers had not cleared the area, which had been the tactic prior to this operation. There were very few German heavy weapons in the landing zone, only a single 88mm flak gun, and the opposition came mainly from support troops of the 84th Infantry Division. Opposition was gradually overcome, mostly by the 139th Engineer Battalion that had been landed by the gliders. By evening, German losses in LZ N were tallied at 83 dead and 315 captured.

The paratroop and glider missions were completed by 1300hrs and were followed by a mission of 240 B-24 bombers dropping a further 582 tons of supplies. The combined US transport total was 8,731 paratroopers, and 4,810 glider troops, and Operation *Varsity* as a whole had involved 17,000 airborne troops delivered into an area of about 25 square miles in four hours. Gen. Ridgway later concluded that "the concept and planning were sound and thorough, and execution flawless. The impact of the airborne divisions, at one blow, completely shattered the hostile defenses, permitting prompt link-up with the assaulting XII Corps, 1 Commando Brigade and Ninth Army to the south." The 17th Airborne Division effectively shattered the German 84th Division and, on D+1, mopped up the landing area and pushed the defensive line over the Issel River up to the autobahn to the east. By March 27, German defenses in this sector had largely collapsed, and the British 6th Guards Armoured Brigade moved through the 17th Armored Division positions, with some US troops riding the British tanks into Dorsten.

Casualties in Operation *Varsity* were moderate due to the crumbling German defenses and the 17th Airborne Division suffered 1,584 casualties including 223 killed, 695 wounded and 666 missing through to March 27, 1945. Operation *Varsity* was instrumental in disrupting German defenses around Wesel, and subsequently permitted the US Ninth Army to inject the 2nd Armored Division north of the Ruhr industrial zone. This maneuver was a key ingredient in the rapid envelopment of the Ruhr by two US armored thrusts, trapping most of the Wehrmacht's Army Group B and ensuring the collapse of German defenses in the west.

XI Troop Carrier Command, Operation *Varsity* March 24, 1945

Unit	Aircraft type	Sorties	Effective	Lost	Troops delivered	Supplies delivered (tons)
Pathfinder Group	C-47	46	46	0	694	18.6
50th TCW	C-47	306	304	5	0	0
50th TCW	CG-4A	377	374	3	1,583	449
52nd TCW	C-47	322	320	14	3,837	130.2
52nd TCW	C-46	73	72	1	2,049	62.9
52nd TCW	CG-4A	80	80	0	200	113.2
53rd TCW	C-47	408	405	11	2,151	130.4
53rd TCW	CG-4A	451	431	20	3,027	449.8
Sub-total (aircraft)		1,155	1147	31	8,731	342.1
Sub-total (glider)		908	885	23	4,810	1,012
Total		2,063	2,032	54	13,541	1,354.1

Proposed 1945 airborne missions				
Codename	Planned date	Drop zone	Airborne unit	Mission
Arena	March 1945	Kassel	four airborne, six air-landing divisions	Create "New Front"
Amherst	April 1945	Netherlands	one British airborne unit	Assist 21st AG advance
Choker II	March–April 1945	Worms	13th Airborne Division	Assist Seventh Army over the Rhine
Eclipse	April 1945	Berlin	Several divisions	Take over Berlin airports in event of government collapse
Effective	April 22, 1945	Stuttgart	13th Airborne Division	Assist advance
Jubiliant	April 1945	Various	1+ divisions	Seize POW camps to prevent atrocities

Although Operation *Varsity* was by far the best organized and best executed of the wartime airborne operations, it was in other respects the least ambitious. By this stage of the war, the German Army was in serious decline and the operation was conducted against a German force already decimated in previous fighting. The airborne force was landed so close to Allied lines that the first link-ups occurred within hours of landing. It is by no means clear that such an elaborate operation was really needed as similar river-crossing operations were conducted along the US Army fronts further to the south without particular difficulty due to the continuing disintegration in the German defenses.

In the wake of the *Varsity* success, First Airborne Army kept the newly arrived 13th Airborne Division ready for Operation *Choker II*, the long-delayed mission to assist the US Seventh Army with a drop behind the Rhine around Mainz; it was canceled on April 4 due to the rapid ground advance and replaced by Operation *Effective*, a proposed drop into the Black Forest area. In early April, the imminent collapse of the Third Reich led Eisenhower's headquarters to give Operation *Jubilant*, a POW rescue mission, precedence over Operation *Eclipse*, a potential Berlin mission. In the event, none of these operations were necessary due to the collapse of German defenses after the encirclement of the Wehrmacht's Army Group B in the Ruhr in mid-April and the collapse of Army Group G in the Saar. On May 4, Brereton's headquarters was asked to prepare a possible mission to land an airborne regiment near Copenhagen to capture the city in advance of the Red Army, but it was canceled due to reports that local forces had surrendered.

Insignia (left to right): 82nd Airborne Division, 101st Airborne Division, 17th Airborne Division, IX Troop Carrier Command.

Assessing the combat record

In the years immediately after the war, the US Army assessed the airborne missions to determine whether or not to maintain the airborne divisions during the inevitable demobilization of much of the army. There were serious proposals to abandon airborne divisions in favor of assigning this mission to normal infantry divisions. Many senior US commanders felt that the airborne division structure was seriously flawed, being much too light to conduct prolonged operations after the initial airdrop. They preferred to assign the task to regular infantry divisions, which would receive additional training for the airborne mission. Even Gen. Gavin admitted that airborne operations were still in their infancy and that "we have barely begun to solve the problems of airborne transport and equipment."

In the event, the army decided to try to correct the organizational flaws in the divisions rather than eliminate them entirely. The underlying problem of the division was the mistaken doctrinal concept that the airborne division would be rapidly extracted from the combat zone a few days after the airborne operation. It was evident from the World War II experience that this precept was unrealistic and that field commanders were not about to relinquish a highly capable light infantry division because of a contrived doctrine. From an organizational standpoint, the senior airborne commanders recommended that the problem could be most readily addressed by re-configuring the airborne divisions like regular infantry divisions, with the full array of supporting troops, instead of the emaciated support structure of the wartime organization. They also recommended that the tables of equipment be modified to permit the substitution of lightweight weapons suitable for air delivery depending on the operational circumstances. So for example, the division would maintain the standard infantry field artillery piece, the 105mm howitzer, but also have a substitute 75mm pack howitzer for airborne operations. There was also general agreement that the distinction between parachute and glider infantry be abandoned and that all infantry be trained for parachute drops.

The glider fell out of favor after the war except where needed for delivering heavy equipment. They were expensive, and wartime experience showed that they were not reusable. Furthermore, they required extremely large air bases to launch on large-scale missions, and they required two highly trained aircrews, the transport tug and glider crew, to carry a single load. Glider missions took up about 50 percent more airspace and flew at speeds 30–40 miles per hour slower than paratroop formations, and so reduced the pace of the airborne assault. The development of larger transport aircraft such as the C-82 permitted the use of pallet loads with large parachutes so that even heavy equipment could be parachuted.

The postwar reassessment also considered the future of airborne operations and their potential role in future wars. There was no consensus on the importance of their future roles. Some commanders hoped that future airborne operations might be large enough to rival the amphibious operations of World War II and have operational rather than mere tactical consequences. Other officers were skeptical that such operations could ever succeed given the need to supply such operations from the air with all the weaknesses and vulnerabilities that it implied. Other officers argued that with the advent of atomic weapons, the days of light infantry were numbered and the future was in the heavy mechanized division that could survive on the nuclear battlefield.

Due to the heavy cuts in force structure after World War II, only two of the five airborne divisions raised during the war were preserved. The exemplary combat record of the 82nd and 101st Airborne Divisions made them virtually sacrosanct in all the postwar cuts and Cold War reorganizations. The airborne divisions were further protected by the rise of several of the airborne generals to senior Army commands, notably Ridgway, Taylor and Gavin. Indeed, the rise of "airborne generals" in the 1950s had some curious effects on US Army Cold War reorganization. Recalling the advantages of the five battlegroups made possible by the use of five regiments in the airborne divisions during Operation *Neptune*, the airborne generals were instrumental in advocating the "Pentomic Division" reorganization of the 1950s that moved away from the US Army's traditional preference for a triangular organization.

The 82nd and 101st Airborne Divisions have remained in the US Army order of battle ever since World War II. By the 1960s, the maturation of the helicopter offered another means of airborne delivery and the 101st was converted to "airmobile," with the 82nd remaining the army's sole airborne division up to the present. The airborne divisions survived and prospered for the past half-century due to the versatility and adaptability of this elite force. For nearly four decades, the armies of NATO and the Warsaw Pact were stalemated along the Central European frontier by the threat of uncontrolled nuclear escalation. The airborne divisions shifted their focus to become the masters of the "little wars" that popped up around the globe. With the end of the Cold War, these light-infantry special-warfare capabilities have become all the more relevant.

Unit status

82nd Airborne Division

The 82nd Division was raised in March 1942 and was initially under the command of Maj. Gen. Omar Bradley. It was converted to an airborne division in August 1942 and by then was under the command of Maj. Gen. Matthew Ridgway. The division landed in North Africa in May 1943 for further training prior to commitment to the invasion of Sicily. The 504th and 505th PIR took part in Operation *Husky* in July 1943 on Sicily. During Operation *Avalanche*, the 504th PIR parachuted into Salerno in September 1943 while the 325th GIR was landed from ship as reinforcements. The 82nd Airborne Division moved to the ETO in December 1943, though the 504th PIR remained in combat on the Italian front, including participation in the Anzio campaign, until late March 1944 when it finally rejoined the division.

For Operation *Neptune*, the division deployed the veteran 505th PIR and 325th GIR, with the addition of the new 507th and 508th PIR in the Normandy drops. By the time of Operation *Market* in September 1944, the order of battle reverted back to the core 504th and 505th PIR and 325th GIR. The 508th PIR remained with the division for this mission and its later wartime assignments, but the 507th PIR was separated and later attached to the 17th Airborne Division. During the Battle of the Bulge, the 517th PIR was under divisional command, but it reverted back to the 11th Airborne Division for the final months of the war.

The 82nd Airborne saw 422 days in combat of which 157 were connected with its four airborne missions (Sicily, Salerno, Normandy, Netherlands) and 265 in ground deployment (Italy, Ardennes, Germany).

Organic units
325th Glider Infantry Regiment
504th Parachute Infantry Regiment
505th Parachute Infantry Regiment
507th Parachute Infantry Regiment (January 14, 1944–August 1944)
508th Parachute Infantry Regiment (January 14, 1944–end of war)
517th Parachute Infantry Regiment (January 1, 1945–February 10, 1945)
319th Glider Field Artillery Battalion
320th Glider Field Artillery Battalion
376th Parachute Field Artillery Battalion
456th Parachute Field Artillery Battalion
80th Airborne Antiaircraft Battalion
307th Airborne Engineer Battalion
307th Airborne Medical Company
82nd Airborne Signal Company
782nd Airborne Ordnance Maintenance Company
407th Airborne Quartermaster Company
82nd Parachute Maintenance Company

82nd Airborne Division attachments, Operation *Neptune*, June–July 1944

Troop B, 4th Cavalry Reconnaissance Squadron	June 1–23
87th Armored Field Artillery Battalion	June 1–8
C/746th Tank Battalion	June 1–11
A/746th Tank Battalion	June 13–21
A/712th Tank Battalion	1–8 July
188th Field Artillery Battalion	June 12–July 8
172nd Field Artillery Battalion	June 16–19
C/899th Tank Destroyer Battalion	June 1–19
A/607th Tank Destroyer Battalion	June 19–July 4
801st Tank Destroyer Battalion	June 30–July 1
803rd Tank Destroyer Battalion	July 1–8
B/87th Chemical Mortar Battalion	June 15–21
D/86th Chemical Mortar Battalion	July 1–4
3809th Quartermaster Truck Company	
3810th Quartermaster Truck Company	
1/603rd Quartermaster Company (GR)	
1/464th Ambulance Company, 31st Medical Group	
493rd Collecting Company, 179th Medical Battalion	
374th Collecting Company, 50th Medical Battalion	
429th Litter Bearing Platoon	
591st Collecting Company	

82nd Airborne Division attachments, Operation *Market*, September 1944

A/50th Field Hospital	September 17–November
666th Quartermaster Truck Company	September 19–November
1st Battalion Coldstream Guards*	September 19–22
5th Battalion Coldstream Guards*	September 19–22
2nd Battalion Irish Guards*	September 19–22
Nottinghamshire Yeomanry (Sherwood Rangers)*	September 19–October 10
1st Royal Dragoons (armoured car)*	September 19–October 10
1st Polish Parachute Brigade	September 25–30
231st Brigade*	September 30–October 1
32nd Guards Infantry Brigade*	September 30–October 1
5th Battalion Coldstream Guards*	September 30–October 10
79th Field Regiment, RA*	September 30–October 230
4th Battery, 54th Anti-tank Regt, RA*	September 30–October 3
130th Infantry Brigade*	October 5–6
2nd Battalion Grenadier Guards*	October 6–7
13/18th Hussars (Queen Mary's Own)*	October 10–November 10

British Army

101st Airborne Division

The 101st Airborne Division was raised at Camp Claiborne, Louisiana, in August 1942 under the command of Maj. Gen. William Lee and based around the 327th and 401st GIR and the 502nd PIR. Maj. Gen. Maxwell Taylor took over command in March 1944 after Gen. Lee suffered a heart attack. For the Normandy landings, the division was substantially reinforced and consisted of two glider regiments (327th and 401st) and three parachute regiments (501st, 502nd, 506th). At the time of Operation *Market*, the division retained this same heavy, five glider/parachute regiment configuration. When committed to defend Bastogne in December 1944, the two glider infantry regiments remained behind in France for refitting and the 401st GIR was subsequently disbanded with assets going to the 327th GIR. As a result, the division in the Ardennes was based around three parachute infantry regiments. It was reinforced with the 509th Parachute Infantry Battalion, a combat-experienced unit that was formerly 2/509th

Organic units
327th Glider Infantry Regiment
401st Glider Infantry Regiment (disbanded March 1, 1945)
501st Parachute Infantry Regiment (January 1944–end of war)
502nd Parachute Infantry Regiment
506th Parachute Infantry Regiment (September 1943–end of war)
321st Glider Field Artillery Battalion
907th Glider Field Artillery Battalion
377th Parachute Field Artillery Battalion
463rd Parachute Field Artillery Battalion
81st Airborne Antiaircraft Battalion
326th Airborne Engineer Battalion
326th Airborne Medical Company
101st Airborne Signal Company
801st Airborne Ordnance Maintenance Company
426th Airborne Quartermaster Company
101st Parachute Maintenance Company

101st Airborne Division attachments, Operation *Neptune*, June 1944
Troop C, 4th Cavalry Squadron
3807th Quartermaster Truck Company
3808th Quartermaster Truck Company
2/Quartermaster Company (GR)
491st Medical Collection Company
Armored Field Artillery Battalion
Tank Destroyer Battalion
759th Tank Battalion

PIR during the fighting in Italy in 1943–44. After being reorganized as a separate battalion, the 509th PIB had taken part in the invasion of southern France as part of the 1st Airborne Task Force.

17th Airborne Division

The 17th Airborne Division was raised in April 1943 at Camp Mackall, North Carolina, under the command of Maj. Gen. William Miley. It originally included the 193rd and 194th GIR along with the 517th PIR, but was substantially reconfigured in 1944 to conform to the two parachute/one

Organic units
194th Glider Infantry Regiment
507th Parachute Infantry Regiment
513th Parachute Infantry Regiment
680th Glider Field Artillery Battalion
681st Glider Field Artillery Battalion
464th Parachute Field Artillery Battalion
466th Parachute Field Artillery Battalion
155th Airborne Antiaircraft Battalion
139th Airborne Engineer Battalion
224th Airborne Medical Company
517th Airborne Signal Company
717th Airborne Ordnance Maintenance Company
411th Airborne Quartermaster Company
17th Parachute Maintenance Company

17th Airborne Division attachments, Operation *Varsity*, March 1945
1 Commando Brigade*
771st Tank Battalion
605th Tank Destroyer Battalion (three in towed guns with 55 DUKW amphibious trucks)
692nd Field Artillery Battalion (25-pdr)
387th Anti-aircraft Artillery Automatic Weapons Battalion
A/3rd Chemical Battalion (Motorized, 4.2in. mortar)
AT Battery (17-pdr)*
53rd (Wessex) Division RA*
81st Field Regiment*
83rd Field Regiment*
133rd Field Regiment*
17th AT Regiment*
25th Light AA Regiment, RA*
77th Medium Regiment, 8th AGRA*
Battery, 382nd Heavy AA Regiment, RA*
British Army

glider regiment configuration. The division swapped the 513th for the 517th PIR in March 1944 and added the 507th PIR in August 1944. The 507th PIR had served with the 82nd Airborne Division in Normandy, so its addition gave the division some needed experience. During the crisis in the Ardennes in December 1944, the division was rushed to the ETO and first served in a defensive line along the Meuse before being committed to combat for the first time on January 3,1945, northwest of Bastogne. It returned to theater reserve on February 10, 1945, in preparation for Operation *Varsity*. At this time, it reorganized under the new December 1944 tables, with the 193rd GIR disappearing and remaining assets being merged into the 194th GIR. The division landed near Wesel on March 24 for Operation *Varsity* and remained in combat in Germany, taking part in the reduction of the Ruhr pocket.

13th Airborne Division

The 13th Airborne Division was raised in August 1943 at Ft. Bragg, North Carolina, under the command of Maj. Gen. George Griner. It was reorganized several times in 1943 before adopting the configuration listed above. It deployed to the ETO in February 1945. The division as a whole did not see combat in the ETO in World War II. However, its 517th PIR was a combat-experienced unit, having been deployed in combat in Italy in May 1944, taken part in the airborne landings in southern France on August 15, 1945, as part of the 1st Airborne Task Force, and been attached to the 82nd Airborne Division during the fighting in the Ardennes. It was attached to the 13th Airborne Division on March 1, 1945, in anticipation of Operation *Choker II*, which never took place.

Organic units
326th Glider Infantry Regiment
515th Parachute Infantry Regiment
517th Parachute Infantry Regiment
676th Glider Field Artillery Battalion
677th Glider Field Artillery Battalion
458th Parachute Field Artillery Battalion
460th Parachute Field Artillery Battalion
153rd Airborne Antiaircraft Battalion
129th Airborne Engineer Battalion
222nd Airborne Medical Company
513th Airborne Signal Company
713th Airborne Ordnance Maintenance Company
409th Airborne Quartermaster Company
13th Parachute Maintenance Company

1st Provisional Airborne Task Force (Seventh Army Provisional Airborne Division)

This provisional unit was formed in July 1944 to conduct the airborne missions included in Operation *Dragoon*, the invasion of southern France. The unit was under the command of Maj. Gen. Robert Frederick who had previously led the Canadian–American 1st Special Services Force ("Devil's Brigade"). Following the airdrops of August 15, 1944, the task force took part in the advance on

Cannes. When the British brigade was removed in August, it was replaced by the 1st SSF. It continued the advance towards the Italian frontier, and reached it on September 8, 1944. At that point, the task force was assigned defensive positions in the Alps along the Franco-Italian border.

Organic units
British 2nd Independent Parachute Brigade (August 15–24, 1944)
517th Parachute Infantry Regiment (to November 22, 1944)
1/551st Parachute Infantry Regiment
509th Parachute Infantry Battalion
550th Glider Infantry Battalion
602nd Field Artillery Battalion
460th Parachute Field Artillery Battalion
463rd Parachute Field Artillery Battalion
596th Airborne Engineer Battalion
887th Airborne Engineer Aviation Company
676th Medical Collecting Company
512th Airborne Signal Company
334th Quartermaster Depot Supply Company

Further reading

Elite formations such as the airborne divisions attract a disproportionate amount of attention in published military accounts. There are dozens, if not hundreds, of memoirs and combat accounts of paratrooper actions in World War II. These are reinforced by scores of other books dealing with paratrooper uniforms and equipment, as well as photographic accounts. The list below can only cover a few of these and concentrates on historical studies. Besides published accounts, there are a wealth of wartime after-action reports and other studies on the airborne operations that are more difficult to find except at archives. The author consulted the collections at the Military History Institute (MHI) at the Army War College at Carlisle Barracks, Pennsylvania, and the US National Archives and Records Administration (NARA) at College Park, Maryland. MHI is a particularly rich repository of archival holdings relating to the airborne including an extensive collection of TO&Es, after-action reports, and personal papers and photos of key commanders including Gen. Ridgway and Gavin, and army historian S. L. A. Marshall.

Official studies and reports

IX Troop Carrier Command, Tactical and Non-Tactical Operations during the Final Phase of the War in Europe including Operation Varsity (1945)

IX Troop Carrier Command, Activities: Final Phase—European War (1945)

17th Airborne Division, Operation Varsity (1945)

101st Airborne Division, Vital Statistics of the 101st Airborne Division in Holland and Belgium 1944–45 (1945)

82nd Airborne Division, Operation Neptune: Normandy 6 June–8 July 1944 (1944)

82nd Airborne Division, A Graphic History of the 82nd Airborne Division, Operation Market, Holland, 1944 (1944)

British Army of the Rhine. Battlefield Tour: Operation Varsity (1947)

USAAF, Airborne Assault on Holland: An Interim Report (1945)

USAAF Evaluation Board, The Effectiveness of Third Phase Tactical Air Operations in the European Theater 5 May 1944–8 May 1945 (1945)

USAF Historical Study No. 36, Ninth Air Force: April to November 1944 (1947)

USAF Historical Study No. 47, Development and Procurement of Gliders in the Army Air Forces 1941–44 (1947)

USAF Historical Study No. 74, Airborne Missions in the Mediterranean 1942–45 (1955)

USAF Historical Study No. 97, Airborne Operations in World War II: European Theater (1957)

USFET General Board, Types of Divisions—Post-War Army (US Army 1945)

USFET General Board, Organization, Equipment and Tactical Employment of the Airborne Division (1945)

Books

Adelman, Robert, and Walton, George, The Champagne Campaign: The Spectacular Airborne Invasion that Turned the Tide of Battle in Southern France in 1944 Little, Brown: 1969

Anzuoni, Robert, "I'm the 82nd Airborne Division": A History of the All American Division in World War II in After Action Reports Schiffer: 2006

Bando, Mark, 101st Airborne: The Screaming Eagles at Normandy MBI: 2001

Bilstein, Roger, *Airlift and Airborne Operations in World War II* USAF History
    Program: 1998

Blair, Clay, *Ridgway's Paratroopers: The American Airborne in World War II*
    Dial: 1985

Blythe, William, *The 13th Airborne Division* Atlanta: 1945

Brereton, Lewis, *The Brereton Diaries* Morrow: 1946

Dawson, W. Forrest., *The Saga of the All-Americans: the 82nd Airborne Division*
    82nd Div. Assoc. 1946; Battery Press reprint

Deschodt, Christophe, and Rouger, L., *D-Day Paratroopers*: *The Americans*
    Histoire & Collections: 2004

Devlin, Gerard, *Paratrooper: The Saga of Army and Marine Parachute and Glider
    Combat Troops in World War II* St. Martin's: 1985

Devlin, Gerard, *Silent Wings: The Saga of Army and Marine Combat Glider Pilots
    during World War II* St. Martin's: 1979

Esvelin, Philippe, *D-Day Gliders, Les planeurs Americans du Jour* J Heimdal: 2002

Gavin, James, *On to Berlin: Battles of an Airborne Commander 1943–46*
    Viking: 1978

Hamlin, John, *Support and Strike: A Concise History of the US Ninth Air Force
    in Europe* GMS: 1987

Hays, J. J., *US Army Ground Forces Tables of Organization and Equipment World
    War II: The Airborne Division 1942–1945 Volumes 3/I and 3/II* Military
    Press: 2003

Huston, James, *Out of the Blue: US Army Airborne Operations in World War II*
    Purdue University: 1972

Isby, David, *C-47/R4D Units of the ETO and MTO* Osprey: 2005

Koskimaki, George, *D-Day with the Screaming Eagles* 1970; Casemate
    reprint: 2002.

Margry, Karel (ed.), *Operation Market-Garden: Then and Now* 2 vol., After the
    Battle: 2002

Marshall, S. L. A., *Night Drop: The American Airborne Invasion of Normandy*
    Little, Brown: 1962

Masters, Charles J., *Glidermen of Neptune* S. Illinois University Press, 1995

Mrazek, James, *The Glider War* St. Martin's: 1975

Nordyke, Phil, *All American-All the Way: The Combat History of the 82nd
    Airborne Division in World War II* Zenith: 2005

Pay, Don, *Thunder from Heaven: The Story of the 17th Airborne Division 1943–45*
    1947; Battery Press reprint: 2001

Rapaport, Leonard, and Northwood, A., *Rendezvous with Destiny: The 101st
    Airborne Division* Infantry Journal 1947; Battery Press reprint

Saunders, Tim, *Battleground Europe: Hell's Highway–US 101st Airborne Division
    & Guards Armoured Division* Leo Cooper: 2001

Saunders, Tim, *Battleground Europe: Nijmegen–US 82nd Airborne and Guards
    Armoured Division* Leo Cooper: 2001

Shama, H. Rex, *Pulse and Repulse: Troop Carrier and Airborne Teams in Europe
    during World War II* Eakin: 1995

Taylor, Maxwell, *Swords and Plowshares* Norton: 1972

Wolfe, Martin, *Green Light: A Troop Carrier Squadron's War from Normandy
    to the Rhine* Univ. Of Pennsylvania: 1983

Young, Charles, *Into the Valley: The Untold Story of the USAAF Troop Carrier
    in World War II* PrintComm: 1995

Glossary

AAF	Army Air Force
AEAF	Allied Expeditionary Air Force
AGF	Army Ground Forces
CG-4A	Combat glider-4A, often called "Waco" after the firm which designed it.
DZ	Drop zone (paratroops)
EM	Enlisted men
ETO	European theater of operations
ETOUSA	European theater of operations—US Army
FAAA	First Allied Airborne Army
GIR	Glider infantry regiment
IP	Initial point; point from which an aerial formation sets the final course to their objective
LZ	Landing zone (gliders)
PIR	Parachute infantry regiment
SHAEF	Supreme Headquarters, Allied Expeditionary Force, led by Gen. Dwight Eisenhower
TCG	Troop carrier group
TCS	Troop carrier squadron
TCW	Troop carrier wing
TO	Table of organization
TO&E	Table of organization and equipment; began to supersede TO after July 1943

Index